INSPIRATION

INSPIRATION

Prof. ARCHIBALD A. HODGE, D.D., LL.D.

AND

Prof. BENJAMIN B. WARFIELD, D.D.

Introduction by
ROGER R. NICOLE

BAKER BOOK HOUSE
Grand Rapids, Michigan

*Reprinted from the 1881 edition
published by Presbyterian
Board of Publication*

*Paperback edition issued 1979
by Baker Book House*

ISBN: 0-8010-4222-4

*Introduction and appendixes 3-6
by Roger R. Nicole
copyrighted 1979 by
Baker Book House Company*

CONTENTS

INTRODUCTION

The work that is hereby made again available to the public appeared originally in the *Presbyterian Review* for April 1881, was reprinted the same year in Philadelphia, and was further reprinted in Glasgow in 1891 in a volume of essays on *The Westminster Doctrine Anent Holy Scripture*.[1] This paper represents a remarkable concurrence between two former students of Charles Hodge, and it stands at a critical point in the history of rather protracted debates that shook the Presbyterian Church in the U.S.A. in the last two decades of the nineteenth century.[2]

The first author, Archibald Alexander Hodge (1823-1886), was in 1881 at the apex of a very meaningful and

1. "Inspiration," *Presbyterian Review* 2 (1881): 225-60; *Inspiration* (Philadelphia: Presbyterian Board of Publication, 1881); Robert Howie, ed., *The Westminster Doctrine Anent Holy Scripture: Tractates by A. A. Hodge and Warfield, with Notes on Recent Discussions* (Glasgow: Bryce, 1891). It is the second of the three that serves as the basis for the present reprinting.

2. For a very stimulating and well-documented account of the theological controversies in the Presbyterian Church in the U.S.A. since 1869, consult Lefferts A. Loetscher, *The Broadening Church: A Study of Theological Issues in the Presbyterian Church Since 1869* (Philadelphia: University of Pennsylvania, 1954). Although Loetscher viewed that to be a desirable "broadening" of the church, which Hodge and Warfield (and

effective teaching career. After completing his course of studies at Princeton Theological Seminary, being notably exposed to the teaching of his own father, Charles Hodge, he had first served for a season as a missionary in India (1847-1851). Compelled to return to the United States because of the failing health of both himself and his wife, he served with distinction as a pastor in three charges. In 1864 he was called to become professor of systematic theology at the seminary in Allegheny, Pennsylvania (now merged with others under the name Pittsburgh Theological Seminary). He served there until 1877 when he was called to be associated with his own father at the Princeton seminary. The joint labors lasted only a very limited time, for Charles died in June 1878; his son succeeded him in the chair of theology. This tenure also was short, for Archibald himself died at the end of 1886 at age 63.

At several points in his literary career, Hodge had presented in print his view of the doctrine of Scripture, most notably in *Outlines of Theology* (1860), pages 67-89; and *A Commentary on the Confession of Faith* (1869), pages 43-69. Later, in 1884, he wrote a large article on "The Consensus of the Reformed Confessions," in which his discussion of Scripture occupies pages 282-86.[3]

---

later J. Gresham Machen) had considered a most deplorable "loosening" of its foundation, this study provides a very well-organized guide to this period with abundant references to the primary sources. Whatever may be thought of the merits of their stance, this volume surely manifests that Hodge and Warfield were singularly clear-sighted concerning the direction of the drift of their denomination, and that from their own point of view they had no other option than to resist it with all their strength.

3. *Outlines of Theology* (New York: Carter, 1860); *A Commentary on the Confession of Faith* (Philadelphia: Presbyterian

Further interesting statements on Scripture appear in the following works published posthumously: *Evangelical Theology* (1887), pages 68-93; and *The System of Theology Contained in the Westminster Shorter Catechism* (1888), pages 9-11.[4]

The position espoused in the present work is in perfect consistency with all these statements, and it represents a particularly clear formulation of the view of inspiration held first by Archibald Alexander (Hodge's namesake) and then by Charles Hodge.[5] This position, it is claimed, concurs with the great stream of orthodox Christianity from the time of the apostles, passing through the major leaders of the Reformation.

The second author, Benjamin Breckinridge Warfield (1851-1921), was in 1881 at the threshold of his notable theological career. He had graduated from Princeton Theological Seminary in 1876. After a brief stay in Europe, he was called in 1878 to Western Theological Seminary in Allegheny as an instructor in New Testament. He was promoted to the rank of professor in 1879. Hodge had already left Western when Warfield joined the faculty there. By 1881 Warfield had published little, although his inaugural lecture on "Inspiration and Criti-

Board of Publication, 1869); "The Consensus of the Reformed Confessions," *Presbyterian Review* 5 (1884): 266-304. Later enlarged editions of *Outlines* have the material on Scripture on pages 65-93.

4. *Evangelical Theology: A Course of Popular Lectures* (Philadelphia: Presbyterian Board of Publication, 1887); *The System of Theology Contained in the Westminster Shorter Catechism Opened and Explained* (New York: Armstrong, 1888). In an English edition of *Evangelical Theology*, which is paginated differently, the discussion of Scripture occurs on pages 61-83.

5. Concerning Charles Hodge's doctrine of inspiration and inerrancy, see appendix 5.

cism" had appeared in print. This had shown the direction of Warfield's interest, and yet it was a singular honor for him to be associated with Hodge in this project and to be permitted to contribute the major part of the article.

It may be called the first of an amazing series of writings focusing on the doctrine of inspiration and produced by Warfield between 1880 and 1915, with special concentration in the years 1888-1894. In addition to the three articles included in this volume, eighty-three others are listed in chronological order, and numbered, in appendix 3.

In view of the massive character of this contribution, it is not surprising that the literary heirs of Warfield chose to publish as their first volume a selection of articles on inspiration under the title *Revelation and Inspiration.*[6] This splendid volume of more than 450 pages was the first to go out in print in the ten-volume Oxford series. It is also in this same area that Samuel G. Craig chose to produce the first volume of his series of reprints of Warfield, paralleling very closely the selection of the earlier work.[7]

Various strains in Warfield's production are recognizable:

1. Some articles deal with the total sweep of the doctrine, providing a masterly summary of the whole area (see notably, in addition to the present article, numbers 2, 11, 37, 48, 66, 78, 82, 83 in appendix 3).

2. There are intensive studies of particular biblical expressions carried out with meticulous care and in great detail. This category particularly includes the

6. New York: Oxford University, 1927.

7. *The Inspiration and Authority of the Bible,* ed. Samuel G. Craig (Philadelphia: Presbyterian and Reformed, 1948).

great series of three articles in the *Presbyterian and Reformed Review* (59, 61, 62) and the great study on the word *scripture* in the *Princeton Theological Review* (79).

3. There are studies in the history of the doctrine relating mainly to three themes with which Warfield was especially familiar: Augustine (72, 73), Calvin (76 and, in summary form, 77), and the Westminster Assembly (35, 41; see also 12, 14, 15, 46, prepared for weekly Presbyterian magazines).[8]

4. Although the controversial mood was never far from Warfield's mind, it is especially dominant in many book reviews and in four articles (16, 17, 33, 47).

If we take the size of a page in *Revelation and Inspiration* as a standard and evaluate the length of the contributions listed in appendix 3, we obtain an approximate figure of 1,251 pages, about three times the materials contained in *The Inspiration and Authority of the Bible*.[9] In view of the size and importance of this work,

8. Concerning the view of Scripture affirmed by the Westminster Assembly and the divines who comprised that assembly, see appendix 6.

9. One area that is closely akin to inspiration is that of the canon. We may note the following contributions of Warfield in this realm: "The Apologetical Value of the Testament of the Twelve Patriarchs," *Presbyterian Review* 1 (1880): 57-84; *Syllabus of the Canon of the New Testament in the Second Century* (Pittsburgh, 1881); "The Canonicity of II Peter," *Southern Presbyterian Review* 33 (1882): 45-75; "Dr. Edwin A. Abbott on the Genuineness of II Peter," *Southern Presbyterian Review* 34 (1883): 390-455; "The Christian Canon," *Philadelphia* 1 (1887): 300-304; *The Canon of the New Testament* (Philadelphia: American Sunday School Union, 1892); "Dr. McGiffert's Theory of the Origin of the New Testament Canon," *Presbyterian Journal* 19 (1894): 360, 376-77; review of David S. Muzzey, *The Rise of the New Testament* (1900), in *Presbyterian and Reformed Review* 11 (1900): 712-13.

it is not surprising that a number of scholars have written articles or theses relating to Warfield's view.[10]

In the present work Hodge chose to write the first part on pages 5-29. This section provides a definition of inspiration, a statement of the presuppositions of the doctrine, a discussion of the genesis of the Scripture with special emphasis on the role of the human writers of Scripture in its production, and an extensive and balanced statement in which inspiration is described as plenary and verbal, and in which are discussed the questions of the relation of inspiration to biblical criticism and the extent to which the superintendence of God controlled the writers.

It was left for Warfield to consider the proof of the doctrine, which he surveyed only in the greatest generality, and to discuss the presuppositions under which critical objections must be evaluated. Here a very general statement is made about the authenticity and integrity of the books of the canon and a much more extensive discussion is provided of alleged errors in the Scripture either in historical or geographical statements, or with respect to internal discrepancies, or again with respect to the application of the Old Testament by the New Testament writers. In all of these areas Warfield asserted that no proven error is found, and he supported his position by showing how the alleged difficulties can be resolved in some of the most difficult cases.

This article was the opening salvo in a series of articles published in the *Presbyterian Review* between 1881 and 1883, and destined to air out varying views in the Presbyterian Church in the U.S.A. The rest of the series proceeded as follows: (2) Charles A. Briggs, "Crit-

10. See the bibliography in appendix 4.

ical Theories of the Sacred Scriptures in Relation to Their Inspiration: I. The Right, Duty, and Limits of Biblical Criticism"; (3) William Henry Green, "Professor W. Robertson Smith on the Pentateuch"; (4) Henry Preserved Smith, "The Critical Theories of Julius Wellhausen"; (5) Samuel I. Curtiss, "Delitzsch on the Origin and Composition of the Pentateuch"; (6) Willis J. Beecher, "The Logical Methods of Professor Kuenen"; (7) Charles A. Briggs, "A Critical Study of the History of Higher Criticism with Special Reference to the Pentateuch"; and (8) Francis L. Patton, "The Dogmatic Aspect of Pentateuchal Criticism."[11]

Articles 1, 3, 6, and 8 may be seen as supporting the view of Hodge and Warfield. Articles 2, 4, 5, and 7 were written in the main in defense of the rights of biblical criticism, although at this stage they were marked by very great caution, which some of the writers — notably Smith and Briggs — later substantially abandoned.

Meanwhile in the evangelical world Hodge's and Warfield's article was construed by some as presenting a lowered view of inspiration. It is this kind of criticism to which Warfield was most sensitive, and he was led to publish two clarifications in defense of the portion of the article which had been penned by Hodge. These were published respectively in the *Presbyterian* for 13 August 1881 and in the *Truth* for February 1883, the latter in response to a rather sharp attack by James H. Brookes. Since these pieces are rather elusive, it was deemed desirable to republish them here along with the present article as appendixes 1 and 2.

It appears amazing to us that a production written with such transparent clarity could at all be mis-

11. *Princeton Review:* (2) 2 (1881): 550-79; (3) 3 (1882): 108-56; (4) 3 (1882): 357-88; (5) 3 (1882): 553-88; (6) 3 (1882): 701-31; (7) 4 (1883): 69-130; (8) 4 (1883): 341-410.

construed, and Brookes had the integrity to acknowledge his mistake in this respect. Surely the fault did not
lie with Hodge and Warfield, although the extent to
which they gave room to the exercise of human agency
in the production of Scripture and the clarity with
which they assessed the place of Scripture in the struc-
ture of dogmatics could raise difficulties with conven-
tional orthodoxy, especially as held by less penetrating
thinkers.

It is interesting to note that in the present article the
words *inerrant* and *inerrancy* do not occur, although the
terms *errorless* and *without error* are repeatedly used
by both writers and the whole intent of the article is to
make it clear that the superintendence of God in Scripture guarantees the errorless infallibility of all scriptural affirmations. After almost one hundred years this
article in its main positions has hardly aged. The part
written by Warfield and the detailed discussion of specific problems would, of course, need to be updated, but
it is a tribute to these two scholars that in their defense
of the doctrine and in their grasp of its implications,
they were so far forth right that an evangelical in the
latter part of our century may wholeheartedly assent to
what they said.

ROGER R. NICOLE
Gordon-Conwell Theological Seminary

THE word "Inspiration," as applied to the Holy Scriptures, has gradually acquired a specific technical meaning independent of its etymology. At first this word, in the sense of "God-breathed," was used to express the entire agency of God in producing that divine element which distinguishes Scripture from all other writings. It was used in a sense comprehensive of supernatural revelation, while the immense range of providential and gracious divine activities concerning the genesis of the word of God in human language was practically overlooked. But Christian scholars have come to see that this divine element, which penetrates and glorifies Scripture at every point, has entered and become incorporated with it in very various ways, natural, supernatural and gracious, through long courses of providential leading, as well as by direct suggestion—through the spontaneous action of the souls of the sacred writers, as well as by controlling influence from without. It is important that distinguishable

ideas should be connoted by distinct terms, and
that the terms themselves should be fixed in a
definite sense. Thus we have come to distinguish
sharply between Revelation, which is the fre-
quent, and Inspiration, which is the constant,
attribute of all the thoughts and statements of
Scripture, and between the problem of the genesis of Scripture on the one hand, which includes
historic processes and the concurrence of natural
and supernatural forces, and must account for all
the phenomena of Scripture, and the mere fact
of inspiration on the other hand, or the superintendence by God of the writers in the entire process of their writing, which accounts for nothing
whatever but the absolute infallibility of the
record in which the revelation, once generated,
appears in the original autograph. It will be
observed that we intentionally avoid applying
to this inspiration the predicate "influence." It
summoned, on occasion, a great variety of in-
fluences, but its essence was superintendence.
This superintendence attended the entire process
of the genesis of Scripture, and particularly the
process of the final composition of the record.
It interfered with no spontaneous natural agen-
cies, which were, in themselves, producing results conformable to the mind of the Holy Spirit.
On occasion it summoned all needed divine in-

fluences and suggestions, and it sealed the entire record and all its elements, however generated, with the imprimatur of God, sending it to us as his Word.

The importance of limiting the word "inspiration" to a definite and never-varying sense, and one which is shown, by the facts of the case, to be applicable equally to every part of Scripture, is self-evident, and is emphasized by the embarrassment which is continually recurring in the discussions of this subject, arising sometimes from the wide, and sometimes from the various, senses in which this term is used by different parties. The history of theology is full of parallel instances, in which terms of the highest import have come to be accepted in a more fixed and narrow sense than they bore at first either in scriptural or early ecclesiastical usage, and with only a remote relation to their etymology; as, for instance, Regeneration, Sacrament, etc.

PRESUPPOSITIONS.

From this definition of the term it is evident that instead of being, in the order of thought, the first religious truth which we embrace, upon which, subsequently, the entire fabric of true religion rests, it is the last and crowning attribute of those sacred books from which we derive

our religious knowledge. Very many religious
and historical truths must be established before
we come to the question of inspiration; as, for
instance, the being and moral government of
God, the fallen condition of man, the fact of a
redemptive scheme, the general historical truth
of the Scriptures, and the validity and authority
of the revelation of God's will, which they contain—*i. e.* the general truth of Christianity and
its doctrines. Hence it follows that, while the
inspiration of the Scriptures is true, and, being
true, is a principle fundamental to the adequate
interpretation of Scripture, it nevertheless is not
in the first instance a principle fundamental to
the truth of the Christian religion. In dealing
with skeptics it is not proper to begin with the
evidence which immediately establishes inspiration, but we should first establish theism, then
the historical credibility of the Scriptures, and
then the divine origin of Christianity. Nor
should we ever allow it to be believed that the
truth of Christianity depends upon any doctrine
of inspiration whatever. Revelation came in
large part before the record of it, and the Christian Church before the New-Testament Scriptures.
Inspiration can have no meaning if Christianity
is not true, but Christianity would be true and
divine—and, being so, would stand—even if God

had not been pleased to give us, in addition to his revelation of saving truth, an infallible record of that revelation absolutely errorless by means of inspiration.

In the second place, it is also evident that our conception of revelation and its methods must be conditioned upon our general views of God's relation to the world, and his methods of influencing the souls of men. The only really dangerous opposition to the Church doctrine of inspiration comes either directly or indirectly, but always ultimately, from some false view of God's relation to the world, of his methods of working, and of the possibility of a supernatural agency penetrating and altering the course of a natural process. But the whole genius of Christianity, all of its essential and most characteristic doctrines, presuppose the immanence of God in all his creatures, and his concurrence with them in all of their spontaneous activities. In him, as an active, intelligent Spirit, we all live and move and have our being. He governs all his creatures and all their actions, working in men even to will and spontaneously to do his good pleasure. The currents, thus, of the divine activities do not only flow around us, conditioning or controlling our action from without, but they none the less flow within the inner current of our personal

lives, confluent with our spontaneous self-move-
ments, and contributing to the effects whatever
properties God may see fit that they shall have.

There is also a real logical and ideal, if not a
physical, continuity between all the various prov-
inces and methods of God's working : providence
and grace, the natural and the supernatural, all
constitute one system in the execution of one
plan.   All these agents and all these methods
are so perfectly adjusted in the plan of God that
not one interferes with any other, and all are so
adjusted and controlled as that each works perfectly, according to the law of its own nature,
and yet all together infallibly bring about the
result God designs.   In this case that design is a
record without error of the facts and doctrines
he had commissioned his servants to teach.

Of the manner in which God may inform
and direct a free intelligence without violating
its laws we have a familiar analogy in Nature
in the relation of instinct to free intelligence.
Intelligence is personal, and involves self-con-
sciousness and liberty.   Instinct is impersonal,
unconscious, and not free.   Both exist alike in
man, with whom intelligence predominates, and
in the higher animals, with whom instinct predominates.   In every case the instinct of the
creature is the intelligence of the Creator work-

ing through the creature's spontaneity, informing and directing, yet never violating any of the laws of his free intelligence. And in Nature we can trace this all the way from the instinct of the bee, which works mechanically, to the magic play of the æsthetic instincts, which largely constitute the genius of a great artist. We are not absurdly attempting to draw a parallel between natural instinct and supernatural inspiration. But the illustration is good simply to show that as a matter of fact God does prompt from within the spontaneous activities of his intelligent creatures, leading them by unerring means to ends imperfectly discerned by themselves; and that this activity of God, as in instinct or otherwise, does not in any wise reveal itself, either in consciousness or in the character of the action to which it prompts, as interfering with the personal attributes or the free rational activities of the creature.

THE GENESIS OF SCRIPTURE.

We allude here to this wide and as yet imperfectly explored subject only for the purpose of distinctly setting apart the various problems it presents, and isolating the specific point of inspiration, with which we, as well as the Church in general, are more particularly interested. All

parties of believers admit that this genesis of
Holy Scripture was the result of the co-operation,
in various ways, of the agency of men and the
agency of God.

The human agency, both in the histories out
of which the Scriptures sprang, and in their immediate composition and inscription, is everywhere apparent, and gives substance and form
to the entire collection of writings. It is not
merely in the matter of verbal expression or literary composition that the personal idiosyncra-
sies of each author are freely manifested by the
untrammeled play of all his faculties, but the
very substance of what they write is evidently
for the most part the product of their own mental and spiritual activities. This is true except
in that comparatively small element of the whole
body of sacred writing in which the human authors simply report the word of God objectively
communicated, or, as in some of the prophecies,
they wrote by divine dictation. As the general
characteristic of all their work, each writer was
put to that special part of the general work for
which he alone was adapted by his original en-
dowments, education, special information and
providential position. Each drew from the stores
of his own original information, from the contributions of other men and from all other natural

sources. Each sought knowledge, like all other authors, from the use of his own natural faculties of thought and feeling, of intuition and of logical inference, of memory and imagination, and of religious experience. Each gave evidence of his own special limitations of knowledge and mental power, and of his personal defects as well as of his powers. Each wrote upon a definite occasion, under special historically grouped circumstances, from his own standpoint in the progressively unfolded plan of redemption, and each made his own special contribution to the fabric of God's word.

The divine agency, although originating in a different source, yet emerges into the effect very much through the same channels. The Scriptures have been generated, as the plan of redemption has been evolved, through an historic process. From the beginning God has dealt with man in the concrete, by self-manifestations and transactions. The revelation proceeds from facts to ideas, and has been gradually unfolded as the preparation for the execution of the work of redemption has advanced through its successive stages. The general providence unfolding this plan has always been divine, yet has also been largely natural in its method, while specially directed to its ends, and at the same time surcharged along

2

portions of its line, especially at the beginning and at great crises, with the supernatural, as a cloud is surcharged with electricity. There were divine voices, appearances, covenants, supernatural communications and interventions—the introduction of new institutions, and their growth under special providential conditions. The prophet of God was sent with special revelations and authority at particular junctures to gather and interpret the lessons of the past, and to add to them lessons springing out of the providential conditions of the present. The Script ures were generated through sixteen centuries cf this divinely-regulated concurrence of God and man, of the natural and the supernatural, of reason and revelation, of providence and grace. They are an organism consisting of many parts, each adjusted to all the rest, as the "many members" to the "one body." Each sacred writer was by God specially formed, endowed, educated, providentially conditioned, and then supplied with knowledge naturally, supernaturally or spiritually conveyed, so that he, and he alone, could, and freely would, produce his allotted part. Thus God predetermined all the matter and form of the several books largely by the formation and training of the several authors, as an organist determines the character of his music as much

when he builds his organ and when he tunes his
pipes as when he plays his keys.   Each writer
also is put providentially at the very point of
view in the general progress of revelation to
which his part assigns him.   He inherits all the
contributions of the past.   He is brought into
place and set to work at definite providential
junctures, the occasion affording him object and
motive, giving form to the writing God appoints
him to execute.

The Bible, moreover, being a work of the
Spirit for spiritual ends, each writer was prepared precisely for his part in the work by the
personal dealings of the Holy Spirit with his
soul.   Spiritual illumination is very different
from either revelation or inspiration, and yet it
had, under the providence of God, a large share
in the genesis of Scripture, contributing to it a
portion of that divine element which makes it
the word of God.   The Psalms are divinely-
inspired records of the religious experience of
their writers, and are by God himself author-
itatively set forth as typical and exemplary for
all men for ever.   Paul and John and Peter
largely drew upon the resources and followed the
lines of their own personal religious experience
in the intuitional or the logical development of
their doctrine; and their experience had, of course,

been previously divinely determined for that very purpose. And in determining their religious experience God so far forth determined their contributions to Scripture. And he furnished each of the sacred writers, in addition to that which came to him through natural channels, all the knowledge needed for his appointed task, either by vision, suggestion, dictation or elevation of faculty, or otherwise, according to his will. The natural knowledge came from all sources, as traditions, documents, testimonies, personal observations and recollections — by means also of intuitions, logical processes of thought, feeling, experience, etc.; and yet all were alike under the general direction of God's providence. The supernatural knowledge became confluent with the natural in a manner which violated no law of reason or of freedom. And throughout the whole of his work the Holy Spirit was present, causing his energies to flow into the spontaneous exercises of the writer's faculties, elevating and directing where need be, and everywhere securing the errorless expression in language of the thought designed by God. This last element is what we call "Inspiration."

In all this process, except in a small element of prophecy, it is evident that as the sacred writers were free and active in their thinking and in the expression of their thoughts, so they were conscious of what they were doing, of what their words meant, and of the design of their utterance. Yet, even then, it is no less evident that they all, like other free instruments of Providence, "builded better than they knew." The meanings of their words, the bearing of the principles they taught, of the facts they narrated, and the relation of their own part to the great organism of divine revelation, while luminous to their own consciousness, yet reached out into infinitely wider horizons than those penetrated by any thought of theirs.

STATEMENT OF THE DOCTRINE.

During the entire history of Christian theology the word "Inspiration" has been used to express either some or all of the activities of God co-operating with its human authors in the genesis of Holy Scripture. We prefer to use it in the single sense of God's continued work of superintendence, by which, his providential, gracious and supernatural contributions having been presupposed, he presided over the sacred writers in their entire work of writing, with the design and effect of rendering that writing an errorless record of the matters he designed them to com-

2 *

municate, and hence constituting the entire volume in all its parts the word of God to us.

While we have restricted the word "Inspiration" to a narrower sphere than that in which it has been used by many in the past, nevertheless we are certain that the above statement of the divine origin and infallibility of Scripture accurately expresses the faith of the Christian Church from the first. Still, several points remain to be more particularly considered, concerning which some difference of opinion at present prevails.

First. Is it proper to call this inspiration "plenary"? This word, which has often been made the occasion of strife, is in itself indefinite, and its use contributes nothing either to the precision or the emphasis of the definition. The word means simply "full," "complete," perfectly adequate for the attainment of the end designed, whatever that might have been. There ought not to be on any side any hesitancy to affirm this of the books of the Bible.

Second. Can this inspiration be properly said to be "verbal"? The objection to the application of this predicate to inspiration is urged upon three distinct grounds:

(1.) We believe that the great majority of those who object to the affirmation that inspiration is verbal are impelled thereto by a feeling, more or less definite, that the phrase implies that inspiration is, in its essence, a process of verbal dictation, or that, at least in some way, the revelation of the thought or the inspiration of the writer was by means of the control which God exercised over his words. And there is the more excuse for this misapprehension because of the extremely mechanical conceptions of inspiration maintained by many former advocates of the use of this term "verbal." This view, however, we repudiate as earnestly as any of those who object to the language in question. At the present time the advocates of the strictest doctrine of inspiration in insisting that it is verbal do not mean that in any way the thoughts were inspired by means of the words, but simply that the divine superintendence, which we call inspiration, extended to the verbal expression of the thoughts of the sacred writers, as well as to the thoughts themselves, and that hence the Bible, considered as a record, an utterance in words of a divine revelation, is the word of God to us. Hence, in all the affirmations of Scripture of every kind there is no more error in the words of the original autographs than in the thoughts they were chosen to express. The thoughts and words are both alike human, and therefore subject to human limitations, but the divine superintendence and guarantee extend to the one as much as the other.

(2.) There are others who, while insisting as strongly as any upon the presence of the divine element in Scripture, developed through special providences and gracious dealings, religious experiences and mental processes, in the very manner we have just set forth under the head of the "Genesis of Scripture," yet substantially deny what we have here called "inspiration." They retain the word "inspiration," but signify by it the divine element in the revelation, or providential or gracious dealing aforesaid, and they believe that the sacred writers, having been divinely helped to certain knowledge, were left to the natural limitations and fallibility incidental to their human and personal characters, alike in their thinking out their several narrations and expositions of divine truth, and in their reduction of them to writing. This view gives up the whole matter of the immediate divine authorship of the Bible as the word of God, and its infallibility and authority as a rule of faith and practice. We have only the several versions of God's revelations as rendered mentally and verbally, more or less adequately, yet always imperfectly, by the different sacred writers. This class of

objectors are, of course, self-consistent in reject-
ing verbal inspiration in any sense. But this
view is not consistent either with the claims of
Scripture, the consciousness of Christians or the
historic doctrine of the Church.

(3.) There are others who maintain that the
Scriptures have been certainly inspired so far
forth as to constitute them in all their parts, and
as a whole, an infallible and divinely-authorita-
tive rule of faith and practice, and yet hold that,
while the thoughts of the sacred writers concerning doctrine and duty were inspired and errorless, their language was of purely human suggestion, and more or less accurate. The question
as to whether the elements of Scripture relating
to the course of Nature and to the events of history are without error will be considered below:
it is sufficient to say under the present head that
it is self-evident that, just as far as the thoughts
of Scripture relating to any element or topic
whatsoever are inspired, the words in which
those thoughts are expressed must be inspired
also. Every element of Scripture, whether doctrine or history, of which God has guaranteed
the infallibility, must be infallible in its verbal
expression. No matter how in other respects
generated, the Scriptures are a product of human
thought, and every process of human thought

involves language. "The slightest consideration
will show that words are as essential to intellect-
ual processes as they are t: mutual intercourse.
. . . Thoughts are wedded to words as necessarily as soul to body. Without it the mysteries
unveiled before the eyes of the seer would be
confused shadows; with it, they are made clear
lessons for human life." *

Besides this, the Scriptures are a *record* of
divine revelations, and as such consist of words;
and as far as the record is inspired at all, and as
far as it is in any element infallible, its inspiration must reach to its words. Infallible thought
must be definite thought, and definite thought
implies words. But if God could have rendered the thoughts of the apostles regarding doctrine and duty infallibly correct without words,
and then left them to convey it to us in their
own language, we should be left to precisely that
amount of certainty for the foundation of our
faith as is guaranteed by the natural compe-
tency of the human authors, and neither more
nor less. There would be no divine guarantee
whatever. The human medium would everywhere interpose its fallibility between God and
us. Besides, most believers admit that some of

* Canon Westcott's *Introduction to the Study of the
Gospels*, 5th edition: Introduction, pp. 14, 15.

the prophetical parts of Scripture were verbally
dictated. It was, moreover, promised that the
apostles should speak as the Spirit gave them
utterance. "The word of God came unto the
prophet." The Church has always held, as expressed by the Helvetic Confession, II., "that
the canonical Scriptures *are the word of God.*"
Paul claims that the Holy Spirit superintended
and guaranteed his words as well as his thoughts
(1 Cor. ii. 13). The things of the Spirit we teach
"not in the words which man's wisdom teacheth,
but which the Holy Ghost teacheth" (συγκρίνοντες),
combining spiritual things with spiritual—*i. e.*
spiritual thoughts with spiritual words.

It is evident, therefore, that it is not clearness
of thought which inclines any of the advocates
of a real inspiration of the Holy Scriptures to
deny that it extends to the words. Whatever
discrepancies or other human limitations may
attach to the sacred record, *the line* (of inspired
or not inspired, of infallible or fallible) *can never
rationally be drawn between the thoughts and the
words of Scripture.*

Third. It is asked again : In what way, and to
what extent, is the doctrine of inspiration dependent upon the supposed results of modern
criticism as to the dates, authors, sources and
modes of composition of the several books? To

us the following answer appears to be well founded, and to set the limits within which the Church
doctrine of inspiration is in equilibrium with the
results of modern criticism fairly and certainly :

The doctrine of inspiration, in its essence—
and, consequently, in all its forms—presupposes
a supernatural revelation and a supernatural
providential guidance entering into and determining the genesis of Scripture from the
beginning. Every naturalistic theory, therefore, of the evolution of Scripture, however dis-
guised, is necessarily opposed to any true version of the catholic doctrine of inspiration. It
is also a well-known matter of fact that Christ
himself is the ultimate witness on whose testimony
the Scriptures, as well as their doctrinal contents, rest. We receive the Old Testament just
as Christ handed it to us, and on his authority.
And we receive as belonging to the New Testament all, and only those, books which an apos-
tolically-instructed age testifies to have been produced by the apostles or their companions—i. e.
by the men whom Christ commissioned, and to
whom he promised infallibility in teaching. It
is evident, therefore, that every supposed conclusion of critical investigation which denies the
apostolical origin of a New-Testament book or
the truth of any part of Christ's testimony in

relation to the Old Testament and its contents, or which is inconsistent with the absolute truthfulness of any affirmation of any book so authenticated, must be inconsistent with the true doctrine of inspiration. On the other hand, the defenders of the strictest doctrine of inspiration should cheerfully acknowledge that theories as to the authors, dates, sources and modes of composition of the several books which are not plainly inconsistent with the testimony of Christ or his apostles as to the Old Testament, or with the apostolic origin of the books of the New Testament, or with the absolute truthfulness of any of the affirmations of these books so authenticated, cannot in the least invalidate the evidence or pervert the meaning of the historical doctrine of inspiration.

Fourth. The real point at issue between the more strict and the more lax views of inspiration maintained by believing scholars remains to be stated. It is claimed, and admitted equally on both sides, that the great design and effect of inspiration is to render the Sacred Scriptures in all their parts a divinely infallible and authoritative rule of faith and practice, and hence that in all their elements of thought and expression, concerned in the great purpose of conveying to men a revelation of spiritual doctrine or duty, the

3

Scriptures are absolutely infallible. But if this be so, it is argued by the more liberal school of Christian scholars that this admitted fact is not inconsistent with other facts which they claim are matters of their personal observation: to wit, that in certain elements of Scripture which are purely incidental to their great end of teaching spiritual truth, such as history, natural history, ethnology, archæology, geography, natural science and philosophy, they, like all the best human writings of their age, are, while for the most part reliable, yet limited by inaccuracies and discrepancies. While this is maintained, it is generally at the same time affirmed that when compared with other books of the same antiquity these inaccuracies and discrepancies of the Bible are inconsiderable in number, and always of secondary importance, in no degree invalidating the great attribute of Scripture—its absolute infallibility and its divine authority as a rule of faith and practice.

The writers of this article are sincerely convinced of the perfect soundness of the great catholic doctrine of biblical inspiration—*i. e.* that the Scriptures not only contain, but ARE, THE WORD OF GOD, and hence that all their elements and all their affirmations are absolutely errorless, and binding the faith and obedience of

men.   Nevertheless, we admit that the question
between ourselves and the advocates of the view
just stated is one of fact, to be decided only by
an exhaustive and impartial examination of all
the sources of evidence—*i. e.* the claims and the
phenomena of the Scriptures themselves. There
will undoubtedly be found upon the surface many
apparent affirmations presumably inconsistent
with the present teachings of science, with facts
of history or with other statements of the sacred
books themselves. Such apparent inconsistencies
and collisions with other sources of information
are to be expected in imperfect copies of ancient
writings, from the fact that the original reading
may have been lost, or that we may fail to realize
the point of view of the author, or that we are
destitute of the circumstantial knowledge which
would fill up and harmonize the record. Besides,
the human forms of knowledge by which the
critics test the accuracy of Scripture are themselves subject to error. In view of all the facts
known to us, we affirm that a candid inspection
of all the ascertained phenomena of the original
text of Scripture will leave unmodified the ancient faith of the Church. In all their real
affirmations these books are without error.

It must be remembered that it is not claimed
that the Scriptures, any more than their authors,

are omniscient. The information they convey is in the forms of human thought, and limited on all sides. They were not designed to teach philosophy, science or human history as such. They were not designed to furnish an infallible system of speculative theology. They are written in human languages, whose words, inflections, constructions and idioms bear everywhere indelible traces of human error. The record itself furnishes evidence that the writers were in large measure dependent for their knowledge upon sources and methods in themselves fallible, and that their personal knowledge and judgments were in many matters hesitating and defective, or even wrong. Nevertheless, the historical faith of the Church has always been that all the affirmations of Scripture of all kinds, whether of spiritual doctrine or duty, or of physical or historical fact, or of psychological or philosophical principle, are without any error when the *ipsissima verba* of the original autographs are ascertained and interpreted in their natural and intended sense. There is a vast difference between exactness of statement, which includes an exhaustive rendering of details, an absolute literalness, which the Scriptures never profess, and accuracy, on the other hand, which secures a correct statement of facts or principles intended to be affirmed. It is this accuracy, and this alone, as distinct from exactness, which the Church doctrine maintains of every affirmation in the original text of Scripture without exception. Every statement accurately corresponds to truth just as far forth as affirmed.

PROOF OF THE DOCTRINE.

We of course do not propose to exhibit this evidence in this article. We wish merely to refresh the memory of our readers with respect to its copiousness, variety and cogency.

First. The New-Testament writers continually assert of the Scriptures of the Old Testament, and of the several books which constitute it, that they ARE THE WORD OF GOD. What their writers said God said. Christ sent out the apostles with the promise of the Holy Ghost, and declared that in hearing them men would hear him. The apostles themselves claimed to speak as the prophets of God, and with plenary authority in his name binding all consciences. And while they did so God endorsed their teaching *and their claims* with signs and wonders and divers miracles. These claims are a universal and inseparable characteristic of every part of Scripture.

Second. Although composed by different hu-

3 *

man authors on various subjects and occasions, under all possible varieties of providential conditions, in two languages, through sixteen centuries of time, yet they evidently constitute one system, all their parts minutely correlated, the whole unfolding a single purpose, and thus giving indubitable evidence of the controlling presence of a divine intelligence from first to last.

Third. It is true that the Scriptures were not designed to teach philosophy, science or ethnology, or human history as such, and therefore they are not to be studied primarily as sources of information on these subjects. Yet all these elements are unavoidably incidentally involved in the statements of Scripture. Many of these, because of defective knowledge or interpretation upon our part, present points of apparent confusion or error. Yet the outstanding fact is, that the general conformableness of the sacred books to modern knowledge in all these departments is purely miraculous. If these books, which originated in an obscure province of the ancient world, be compared with the most enlightened cosmogonies or philosophies or histories of the same or immediately subsequent centuries, their comparative freedom even from apparent error is amazing. Who prevented the sacred writers from falling into the wholesale and radical mistakes which were necessarily incidental to their position as mere men? The fact that at this date scientists of the rank of Faraday and Henry, of Dana, of Guyot and Dawson, maintain that there is no real conflict between the really ascertained facts of science and the first two chapters of Genesis, rightly interpreted, of itself demonstrates that a supernatural intelligence must have directed the writing of those chapters. This, of course, proves that the scientific element of Scripture, as well as the doctrinal, was within the scope of inspiration. And this argument is every day acquiring greater force from the results of the critical study of Scripture, and from advanced knowledge in every department of history and science, which continually tend to solve difficulties and to lessen the number of apparent discrepancies.

Fourth. The moral and spiritual character of the revelation which the Scriptures convey of God, of the person of Christ, of the plan of redemption and of the law of absolute righteousness, and the power which the very words of the record, as well as the truths they express, have exercised over the noblest men and over nations and races for centuries,—this is the characteristic self-demonstration of the word of God, and has sufficed to maintain the unabated catholicity of the strict doctrine of inspiration through all change of time and in spite of all opposition.

Fifth. This doctrine of the inspiration of Scripture, in all its elements and parts, has always been the doctrine of the Church. Dr. Westcott has proved this by a copious catena of quotations from Ante-Nicene Fathers in Appendix B to his *Introduction to the Study of the Gospels.* He quotes Clemens Romanus as saying that the Scriptures are " the true utterances of the Holy Ghost." He quotes Tertullian as saying that these books are " the writings and the words of God," and Cyprian as saying that the " gospel cannot stand in part and fall in part," and Clement of Alexandria to the effect that the foundations of our faith " we have received from God through the Scriptures," of which not one tittle shall pass away without being accomplished, " for the mouth of the Lord the Holy Spirit spake it." Dr. Westcott quotes Origen as teaching that the Scriptures are without error, since " they were accurately written by the co-operation of the Holy Ghost," and that the words of Paul are the words of God.

The Roman Church (Can. Conc. Trid., Sess. IV.) says, " God is the author of both " Testaments. The second Helvetic Confession represents the whole Protestant Reformation in saying

(Ch. I.) : " The canonical Scriptures are the true word of God," for " God continues to speak to us through the Holy Scriptures." The Westminster Confession says: " It pleased the Lord at sundry times and in divers manners to reveal himself and to declare his will unto his Church, and afterward . . . to commit the same wholly unto writing." It declares that the Scriptures are in such a sense given by inspiration that they possess a divine authority, and that " God is their author," and they " are the WORD OF GOD."

It is not questionable that the great historic churches have held these creed definitions in the sense of affirming the errorless infallibility of the Word. This is everywhere shown by the way in which all the great bodies of Protestant theologians have handled Scripture in their commentaries, systems of theology, catechisms and sermons. And this has always been pre-eminently characteristic of epochs and agents of reformation and revival. All the great world-moving men, as Luther, Calvin, Knox, Wesley, Whitefield and Chalmers, and proportionately those most like them, have so handled the divine Word. Even if the more lax doctrine has the suffrage of many scholars, or even if it be true, it is nevertheless certain that hitherto in nine-

teen centuries it has never been held by men
who also possessed the secret of using the word
of God like a hammer or like a fire.

LEGITIMATE PRESUMPTIONS.

In testing this question by a critical investigation of the phenomena of Scripture, it is evident that the stricter view, which denies the
existence of errors, discrepancies or inaccurate
statements in Scripture, has the presumption
in its favor, and that the *onus probandi* rests
upon the advocates of the other view. The latter may fairly be required to furnish positive
and conclusive evidence in each alleged instance
of error until the presumption has been turned
over to the other side. The *primâ facie* evidence
of the claims of Scripture is assuredly all in
favor of an errorless infallibility of all scriptural affirmations. This has been from the first
the general faith of the historical Church and of
the Bible-loving, spiritual people of God. The
very letter of the Word has been proved from
ancient times to be a tremendous power in human life.

It is a question also of infinite importance.
If the new views are untrue, they threaten not
only to shake the confidence of men in the
Scriptures, but the very Scriptures themselves

as an objective ground of faith. We have seen
that the Holy Spirit has, as a matter of fact,
preserved the sacred writers to a degree unpar-
alleled elsewhere in literature from error in the
departments of philosophy and science. Who
then shall determine the limit of that preserving
influence? We have seen that in God's plan
doctrine grows out of history, and that redemption itself was wrought out in human history.
If, then, the inspiration of the sacred writers
did not embrace the department of history, or
only of sacred and not of profane history, who
shall set the limit and define what is of the essence of faith and what the uncertain accident?
It would assuredly appear that, as no organism
can be stronger than its weakest part, if error
be found in any one element or in any class of
statements, certainty as to any portion could
rise no higher than belongs to that exercise of
human reason to which it will be left to dis
criminate the infallible from the fallible.

The critical investigation must be made,
and we must abide by the result when it is un-
questionably reached. But surely it must be
carried on with infinite humility and teachable-
ness, and with prayer for the constant guidance
of the gracious Spirit. The signs of success will
never be presumption, an evident sense of intel-

lectual superiority, or a want of sympathy with the spiritual Church of all ages or with the painful confusion of God's humble people of the present.

With these presumptions and in this spirit let it (1) be proved that each alleged discrepant statement certainly occurred in the original autograph of the sacred book in which it is said to be found. (2) Let it be proved that the interpretation which occasions the apparent discrepancy is the one which the passage was evidently intended to bear. It is not sufficient to show a difficulty, which may spring out of our defective knowledge of the circumstances. The true meaning must be definitely and certainly ascertained, and then shown to be irreconcilable with other known truth. (3) Let it be proved that the true sense of some part of the original autograph is directly and necessarily inconsistent with some certainly-known fact of history or truth of science, or some other statement of Scripture certainly ascertained and interpreted. We believe that it can be shown that this has never yet been successfully done in the case of one single alleged instance of error in the WORD OF GOD.

CRITICAL OBJECTIONS TRIED.

It remains only to consider more in detail
some of the special objections which have been
put forward against this doctrine in the name
of criticism. It cannot be, indeed, demanded
that every one urged should be examined and
met, but it may be justly expected that the
chief classes of relevant objections should be
briefly touched upon. This, fortunately, is no
illimitable task. There are, as already stated,
two main presuppositions lying at the base of
the doctrine, essential to its integrity, while to
them it adds one essential supposition. The presuppositions are—1. The possibility of supernatural interference, and the actual occurrence of
that interference in the origin of our Bible;
and, 2. The authenticity, genuineness and historical credibility of the records included in our
Bible. The added supposition is—3. The truth
to fact of every statement in the Scriptures.
No objection from the side of criticism is relevant unless it traverses some one of these three
points. The traditional view of the age and
authorship of a document or of the meaning of
a statement may be traversed, and yet no conflict arise with the doctrine of a strict inspiration. But criticism cannot reach results incon-

4

sistent with the genuineness and authenticity of a
document judged according to the professions of
that document or the statements or implications
of any other part of Scripture, or incompatible
with the truth of any passage in the sense of
that passage arrived at by the correct application of the sound principles of historico-gram-
matical exegesis, without thereby arraying herself in direct opposition to the Church doctrine
of inspiration. All objections to that doctrine
based on such asserted results of criticism are
undoubtedly relevant. Our duty is, therefore,
to ask what results of criticism are claimed
which traverse some one of the three assertions
—of a supernatural origin for the Scriptures,
of genuineness and authenticity for its books,
and of absolute freedom from error of its statements.

1. THE AUTHENTICITY AND INTEGRITY OF THE
    BOOKS OF THE OLD AND NEW TESTA-
    MENTS, AS THEY HAVE COME DOWN TO US.

The first point for us to examine would naturally be the bearing upon the Church doctrine
of inspiration of the various modern critical
theories concerning the origin and present integrity of the several books of the Old and New
Testaments. This is at present the most moment

ous question which agitates the believing world.
The critical examination of all the most inti-
mate phenomena of the text of Scripture is an
obvious duty, and its results, when humility, do-
cility and spiritual insight are added to compe-
tent learning and broad intelligence, must be
eminently beneficial. It is obvious, however,
that this department of the subject could not be
adequately discussed in this paper. It is consequently postponed to the near future, when it
is intended that the whole subject shall be presented as fully as possible.

In the mean time, the present writers, while
they admit freely that the traditional belief as
to the dates and origin of the several books may
be brought into question without involving any
doubt as to their inspiration, yet confidently
affirm that any theories of the origin or authorship of any book of either Testament which
ascribe to them a purely naturalistic genesis,
or dates or authors inconsistent with either their
own natural claims or the assertions of other
Scripture, are plainly inconsistent with the doctrine of inspiration taught by the Church.
Nor have they any embarrassment in the face
of these theories, seeing that they believe them
to rest on no better basis than an over-acute
criticism overreaching itself and building on

fancies. Here they must content themselves with reference to the various critical discussions of these theories which have poured from the press for detailed refutation of them. With this refutation in mind they simply assert their conviction that none of the claims or assertions of the Scriptures as to the authenticity of a single book of either Testament has hitherto been disproved.

II. Detailed Accuracy of Statement.

We are next confronted with objections meant to traverse the third of our preliminary statements, consisting of bold assertions that, whatever may have been their origin, our Scriptures do exhibit phenomena of inaccuracy, that mistakes are found in them, errors committed by them, untrue statements ventured. Nor is this charge put forward only by opponents of revelation: a Van Oosterzee, as well as " a Tholuck, a Neander, a Lange, a Stier," admits " errors and inaccuracies in matters of subordinate importance." * It is plain, however, that if the Scriptures do fail in truth in their statements of whatever kind, the doctrine of inspiration which has been defended in this paper cannot stand. But so long as the principles of historico-

* See Van Oosterzee's *Dogmatics*, p. 205.

grammatical exegesis are relied on to determine
the meaning of Scripture, it is impossible to
escape the fact that the Bible claims to be thus
inspired. And thus it is not a rare thing to find
the very theologians who themselves cannot believe in a strict inspiration yet admitting that
the Scripture writers believed in it.* We cannot, therefore, occupy the ground on which these
great and worthy men seem to us so precariously
to stand. A proved error in Scripture contradicts not only our doctrine, but the Scripture
claims, and therefore its inspiration in making
those claims. It is therefore of vital importance to ask, Can phenomena of error and untruth
be pointed out ?

There is certainly no dearth of " instances "

* Thus Tholuck: " Yet his [the author of Hebrews]
application of the Old Testament rests on the strictest
view of inspiration, since passages where God is not the
speaker are cited as words of God or of the Holy Ghost
(i. 6, 7, 8; iv. 4, 7; vii. 21; iii. 7; x. 15)."—*Old Testament in the New*, in *Bibliotheca Sacra*, xi. p. 612. So also
Richard Rothe: " It is clear, then, that the orthodox theory [*i. e.* the very strictest] of inspiration is countenanced
by the authors of the New Testament." So also Canon
Farrar: " He [Paul] shared, doubtless, in the views of
the later Jewish schools—the Tanaim and Amoraim—
on the nature of inspiration. These views . . . made
the words of Scripture coextensive and identical with
the words of God."—*Life of Paul*, ii p. 47.

4 *

confidently put forward.   But it is abundantly
plain that the vast majority of them are irrelevant.   We must begin any discussion of them,
therefore, by reasserting certain simple propo-
sitions, the result of which will be to clear the
ground of all irrelevant objections.   It is to be
remembered, then, that—1. We do not assert
that the common text, but only that the original
autographic text, was inspired.   No "error" can
be asserted, therefore, which cannot be proved to
have been aboriginal in the text.   2. We do not
deny an everywhere-present human element in
the Scriptures.   No mark of the effect of this
human element, therefore—in style of thought
or wording—can be urged against inspiration
unless it can be shown to result in untruth.   3.
We do not erect inspiration into an end, but hold
it to be simply a means to an end—viz. the accurate conveyance of truth.   No objection, therefore, is valid against the form in which the truth
is expressed, so long as it is admitted that that
form conveys the truth.   4. We do not suppose
that inspiration made a writer false to his professed purpose, but rather that it kept him infallibly true to it.   No objection is valid, therefore, which overlooks the prime question: What
was the professed or implied purpose of the
writer in making this statement?   These few

simple and very obvious remarks set aside the vast
majority of the customary objections. The first
throws out of court numbers of inaccuracies in
the Old and New Testaments as either certainly
or probably not parts of the original text, and
therefore not fit evidence in the case. The
second performs the same service for a still
greater number, which amount simply to the
discovery of individual traits, modes of thought
or expression, or forms of argumentation in the
writings of the several authors of the biblical
books. The third sets aside a vast multitude,
drawn from pressure of language, misreading of
figures, resurrection of the primary sense of
idioms, etc., in utter forgetfulness of the fact that
no one claims that inspiration secured the use of
good Greek in Attic severity of taste, free from
the exaggerations and looseness of current speech,
but only that it secured the accurate expression
of truth, even (if you will) through the medium
of the worst Greek a fisherman of Galilee could
write and the most startling figures of speech a
peasant could invent. Exegesis must be historical as well as grammatical, and must always
seek the meaning *intended*, not any meaning that
can be tortured out of a passage. The fourth in
like manner destroys the force of every objection
which is tacitly founded on the idea that partial

and incomplete statements cannot be inspired, no
documents can be quoted except *verbatim,* no
conversations reported unless at length, etc.,
and which thus denies the right of another to
speak to the present purpose only, appeal to the
sense, not wording of a document, give abstracts
of discourses, and apply, by a true exegesis, the
words of a previous writer to the present need.
The sum of the whole matter is simply this: No
phenomenon can be validly urged against verbal
inspiration which, found out of Scripture, would
not be a valid argument against the truth of the
writing. Inspiration securing no more than this
—*truth,* simple truth—no phenomenon can be
urged against verbal inspiration which cannot be
proved to involve *an indisputable error.*

It is not to be denied that such phenomena are
asserted to be discoverable in the Scriptures. Is
the assertion capable of being supported by facts?
That is the only question now before us. And it
thus becomes our duty to examine some samples
of the chief classes of facts usually appealed to.
These samples—which will, moreover, all be
chosen from the New Testament, and all at the
suggestion of opponents—must serve our present
needs.

HISTORICAL AND GEOGRAPHICAL ACCURACY.

1. It is asserted that the Scripture writers are inaccurate in their statements of historical and geographical facts, as exhibited by the divergence existing between their statements and the information we derive from other sources, such as profane writers and monuments. When we ask for the proofs of this assertion, however, they are found to be very difficult to produce. A generation or two ago this was not so much the case; but the progress of our knowledge of the times and the geography of the region in which our sacred books were written has been gradually wiping out the "proofs" one by one, until they are at this day non-existent. The chief (and almost the only) historical errors still asserted to exist in the New Testament are—the "fifteenth year of Tiberius" of Luke iii. 1; the enrollment during Cyrenius's governorship of Luke ii. 2; and the revolt of Theudas of Acts v. 36. It is not denied that these statements present difficulties, but it is humbly suggested that that is hardly synonymous with saying that they are proved mistakes. *If* Herod died in the spring of A. U. C. 750 (which seems wellnigh certain), and *if*, in Luke iii. 23, the "about" be deemed not broad enough to cover two years (which is

fairly probable), and *if* Luke iii. 1 means to date John's first appearance (as again seems probable), and *if* no more than six months intervened between John's and Jesus' public appearance (which, still again, seems probable),—then it is admitted that the "fifteenth year of Tiberius" must be a mistake—*provided that, still further*, we must count his years from the beginning of his sole reign, and not from his co-regnancy with Augustus; in favor of which latter mode of counting much has been, and more can be, urged. Surely this is not a very clear case of indubitable error, with its *five ifs* staring us in the face. Again, *if* the Theudas mentioned in Acts is necessarily the same as the Theudas mentioned by Josephus, then Luke and Josephus do seem to be in disaccord as to the time of his revolt; and *if* Josephus can be shown to be, in general, a more accurate historian than Luke, then his account must be preferred. But neither of these *ifs* is true. Josephus is the less accurate historian, as is easily proved; and there are good reasons—convincing to a critic like Winer and a Jew like Jost, neither certainly affected by apologetical bias—to suppose that Acts and Josephus mention different revolts. Where, then, is the contradiction?

The greatest reliance is, however, placed on the

third case adduced—the statement of Luke that
Jesus was born at the time of a world-enroll-
ment which was carried out in Syria during the
governorship of Cyrenius. Weiss* offers three
reasons why Luke is certainly incorrect here,
which Schurer† increases to five facts—viz.: 1.
History knows nothing of a general empire-
census in the time of Augustus; 2. A Roman
census would not force Joseph to go to Bethlehem, nor Mary to go with him; 3. Nor could it
have taken place in Palestine in the time of
Herod; 4. Josephus knows nothing of such a
census, but, on the contrary, speaks of that of
Acts v. 37 as something new and unheard of;
and, 5. Quirinius was not governor of Syria during Herod's life. This has a formidable look,
but each detail has been more than fully met.
Thus, Objection 1 turns wholly upon an *argu-
mentum e silentio*, always precarious enough, and
here quadruply so, seeing that (1) an empire-
census is just such a thing as Roman historians
would be likely to omit all mention of, just as
Spatian fails to mention in his life of Hadrian
the famous rescript of that monarch, and all
contemporary history is silent as to Augustus's
geometrical survey; (2) We have no detailed

* Meyer's *Markus und Lukas*, p. 286 (ed. 6).
† *N. T. Zeitgeschichte*, pp. 268–286.

contemporary history of this time, the inaccurate
and gossiping Suetonius and Josephus being our
only sources of information; (3) Certain oft-
quoted passages in Tacitus and Suetonius ac-
quaint us with facts which absolutely require
such a census at their base; and (4) We have
direct, though not contemporary, historical proof
that such a census was taken, in statements of
Cassiodorus and Suidas. Objection 2 gains all
its apparent force from a *confusio verborum.*
Luke does not represent this as a Roman census
in the sense that it was taken up after Roman
methods, but only in the sense that it was ordered
ultimately by Roman authority. Nor does he
represent Mary as being forced to go to Bethlehem with Joseph; her own choice, doubtless, determined her journey. The same *confusio verborum* follows us into Objection 3. It may be
improbable that Herod should have been so far
set aside that a census should have been taken
up in his dominions after Roman methods and
by Roman officials; but is it so improbable that
he should be ordered to take himself a census
after his own methods and by his own officials?
Josephus can give us the answer.* Whatever
may have been Herod's official title, whether *rex*

* Cf. *Ant.*, xv. 10, 4; xvi. 2, 5; 4, 1; 9, 3; xvii. 2, 1;
2, 4; 5, 8; 11, 4, etc., for Herod's status.

socius or, as seems more probable (one stage lower), *rex amicus Cæsaris*, it is certain that he felt bound to bow to the emperor's every whisper; so that if Augustus desired statistics as to the *regna* (and Tacitus proves he did), Herod would be forced to furnish them for his *regnum.* Objection 4 again is easily laid: Josephus not only mentions nothing he could escape which exhibited Jewish subjection, but actually passes over the decade 750–760 so slightly that he can hardly be said to have left us a history of that time. That he speaks of the later census of Acts v. 37 as something new is most natural, seeing that it was, as carried on by the Roman officials and after Roman methods, not only absolutely new, and a most important event in itself, but, moreover, was fraught with such historical consequences that it could not be passed over in silence. Objection 5 is the most important and difficult, but not, therefore, insuperable. It states, indeed, a truth: Quirinius was not governor of Syria until after Herod's death. But it must be noted, on the one hand, that Zumpt has proved, almost, if not quite, to demonstration, that Quirinius was twice governor of Syria, the first time beginning within six months after Herod's death; and, on the other, that Luke does not say that Christ was born while Cyre-

5

nius was governor of Syria.   What Luke says is, that Christ was born during the progress of a census, and then defines the census as the first which was carried on when Cyrenius was governor of Syria.   If this census was begun under Varus and finished under Quirinius, Christ may have been born, according to Luke, at any time during the progress of this census.   This, because Luke ii. 2 is not given to define the time of Christ's birth, but more narrowly to describe what census it was which had in verse 1 been used to define the time of Christ's birth.*   Thus, doubtless, it is true that Christ was born under Varus, and yet during the course of the first Quirinian census; and thus Schürer's fifth objection goes the way of all the others.

The wonderful accuracy of the New-Testa-

---

* Take an example: If one should say of any event, that it occurred during our war with Great Britain, and then add, "I mean that war wherein Jackson fought," would he necessarily refer to an event *late* in the war, after Jackson came to the front?   Not so, because *the war alone* defines the time of the event, and Jackson only *which* war.   So in Luke *the census alone* defines the time of Christ's birth, and Quirinius only *which* census. It ought to be added that there are at least three other methods of explaining Luke's words, all possible, and none very improbable, on the supposition of any one of which conflict with history is impossible.

ment writers in all, even the minute and incidental, details of their historical notices cannot, however, be made even faintly apparent by a simple answering of objections. Some sort of glance over the field as a whole is necessary to any appreciation of it. There occur in the New Testament some thirty names—emperors, members of the family of Herod, high priests, rabbis, Roman governors, princes, Jewish leaders—some mention of which might be looked for in contemporary history or on contemporary monuments.* All but two of these— and they the insignificant Jewish rebels Theudas and Barabbas—are actually mentioned; and the New-Testament notices are found, on comparison, to be absolutely accurate in every, even the most minute, detail. Every one of their statements has not, indeed, passed without challenge,

---

* These are: Augustus, Tiberius, Claudius—Herod Antipas, the two Philips, Archelaus, Agrippa I., Agrippa II., Herodias, Herodias' daughter, Bernice, Drusilla —Annas, Caiaphas, Ananias — Gamaliel — Quirinius, Pilate, Felix, Festus, Gallio, Sergius Paulus—Aretas (Candace), Lysanias—[Theudas], Judas of Galilee [Barabbas]. Candace seems to represent a hereditary title, not a personal name; Theudas and Barabbas are not named in profane sources. Cf. the (incomplete) list and fine remarks of Rawlinson (*Hist. Evidences*, Boston, 1873, p. 195 *sq.*).

but challenge has always meant triumphant
vindication. Some examples of what is here
meant have been given already; others may be
added in a note for their instructiveness.* Now,
the period of which these writers treat is absolutely the most difficult historical period in which to
be accurate that the world has ever seen. Nothing was fixed or stable; vacillation, change, was
everywhere. The province which was senator-
ial to-day was imperial to-morrow—the bound-
aries that were fixed to-day were altered to-morrow. That these writers were thus accurate
in a period and land wherein Tacitus failed to
attain complete accuracy means much.

We reach the same conclusion if we ask after

* It was long boldly asserted that Luke was in error
in making Lysanias a contemporary tetrarch with the
Herodian rulers. But it is now admitted that Josephus
mentions an earlier and a later Lysanias, and so corrobo-
rates Luke; and inscriptions also have been brought forward which supervindicate Luke's accuracy, so that
even M. Renan admits it. Again, it was long contend-
ed that Luke had inaccurately assigned a proconsul to
Cyprus; but this was soon set aside by a reference to
Cyprian coins of Claudius's time and to Dion Cassius,
liv. 4; and now Mr. Cesnola publishes an inscription
which mentions the veritable proconsul Paulus whom
Luke mentioned (*Cyprus*, p. 425). So with reference to
the titles of the rulers of Achaia, Philippi, Ephesus, etc.
(See in general Lee on *Inspiration*, p. 364, note 2.)

their geographical accuracy. In no single case have they slipped here, either; and what this means may be estimated by noting what a mass of geographical detail has been given us.* Between forty and fifty names of countries can be counted in the New-Testament pages; every one is accurately named and placed. About the same number of foreign cities are named, and all equally accurately. Still more to the purpose, thirty-six Syrian and Palestinian towns are named, the great majority of which have been identified,† and wherever testing is possible

---

* Compare the efforts of a real forger with the accuracy of these autoptic writers—*e. g.* of Prochorus, as given in Zahn's *Acta Joannis*, p. lii. Only nine real places can be found in a long list of geographical names invented for the need. Thus, to the little Patmos a number of cities and villages is ascribed which would require a Sicily or Cyprus to furnish ground to stand on.

† These names are: *Ænon, *Antipatris, †Arimathea, *Azotus, *Bethany, †Bethany beyond Jordan, *Bethlehem, ‖Bethphage, ?Bethsaida, ?Cana, ?Capernaum, *Cæsarea, *Cæsarea Philippi, *Chorazin, ‖Dalmanutha, *Damascus, ‡Emmaus, *Ephraim, *Gadara, *Gaza, ?Gerasa, *Jericho, *Jerusalem, *Joppa, †Jouda, †Kerioth, *Lydda, *Magdala, *Nain, *Nazareth, *Salim, *Seleucia, *Sychar, *Tiberias, *Tyre. Those marked * are pretty certainly identified; those †, with great probability; those ?, with a choice between the two places; and those ‖, as to their neighborhood. There are, besides, some names

the most minute accuracy emerges. Whether
due to inspiration or not, this unvarying accuracy of statement is certainly consistent with
the strictest doctrine of inspiration.

COMPLETE INTERNAL HARMONY.

2. Another favorite charge made against these
writers is, that they are often hopelessly inconsistent with one another in their statements; and this
charge of disharmony has sometimes been push-
ed so far as to make it do duty even against
their historical credibility. But when we begin
to examine the instances brought forward in
support of it, they are found to be cases of *difficult*, not of *impossible*, harmony. And it is
abundantly plain that it must be shown to be
impossible to harmonize any two statements on
any natural supposition before they can be asserted to be inconsistent. This is a recognized
principle of historical investigation, and it is
the only reasonable principle possible, unless
we are prepared to assert that the two statements necessarily contain all the facts of the
case and exclude the possibility of the har-

quoted from the Old Testament—*e. g.* ||Gomorrah, *Rama,
*Sarepta, *Shechem, ||Sodom.   Also some other geo
graphical names—*e. g.* *The brook Kedron, *Jordan,
*the Mount of Olives and *the Sea of Galilee, etc.

monizing supposition.   Having our eyes upon
this principle, it is not rash to declare that no
disharmony has ever been proved between any
two statements of the New Testament.   The
best examples to illustrate the character of the
attempts made to exhibit disharmony, and the
rocks on which these attempts always break, are
probably those five striking cases on which Dr.
Fisher most wisely rests his charge against the
complete harmony of the four evangelists—viz.
the alleged disharmony in the accounts of the
place and phraseology of the Sermon on the
Mount, the healing of the centurion's son, the
denials of Peter, the healing of the blind man
at Jericho, and the time of the institution of
the Lord's Supper.*   But that in each of these
most natural means of harmonizing exist, and
are even in some instances recognized as possible by Dr. Fisher himself, President Bartlett has
lately so fully shown in detail † that we cannot
bring ourselves to repeat here the oft-told tale.
Take one or two other examples: for instance,
look at that famous case alleged in the specifi-
cation of the *hour* in John xix. 14 and Mark.
xv. 25.   The difficulty here, says Dean Alford,
is insuperable, and with him Meyer *et al.* agree.

* *Beginnings of Christianity*, p. 460 *sq.*
† *Princeton Review*, January, 1880, p. 47 *sq.*

But even Strauss admits that it would be cancelled "if it were possible to prove that the Fourth Gospel proceeds upon another mode of reckoning time than that used by the Synoptics." And that it is possible to prove this very thing any one can satisfy himself by noting the four places where John mentions the hour (i. 39; iv. 6, 52; xix. 14); whence it emerges that John reckons his hours according to the method prevalent in Asia Minor*—from midnight, and not from daybreak. Thus all difficulty vanishes.†
The disharmony claimed to exist between Matt. xxvii. 6–8 and Acts i. 18, 19 is also voided by a naïve kind of admission; Dean Alford, for instance, asserting in one breath that no reconciliation can be found consistent with common honesty, and in the next admitting that the natural supposition by which the passages are harmonized is "of course possible." This admission, on the recognized principles of historical criticism, amounts simply to a confession that

* That this was the custom in Asia Minor is evident from *Marturium Polyc.*, c. 21, etc. Cf. also (in general) Pliny, *Nat. Hist.*, ii. 77, and Plutarch, *Quaest Rom.*, lxxxiii.

† Cf. Townson's *Discourses*, Discourse 8; McClelland's *N. T.*, vol. i., p. 737 *sq.*; Westcott on *John*, p. 282; Lee on *Inspiration*, p. 352; where this subject is fully discussed.

no disharmony ought to be asserted in the case.

Perhaps, however, the two most important and far-reaching instances of disharmony alleged of late years are—that asserted between the narratives of the events preceding, accompanying and following the birth of our Lord given by Matthew and Luke, which is said to prove the historical untrustworthiness of *both* (!) narratives; and that asserted between the accounts of Paul's visits to Jerusalem and his relations to the Twelve in Acts and Galatians, which is said to prove the unhistorical character of Acts. In the brief space at our disposal it is not possible to disprove such wholesale charges in detail. It must suffice, therefore, to point out the lines on which such a refutation proceeds. In the first instance the charge can be upheld only by the expedient of assuming that silence as to an event constitutes denial of that event, supported by criticisms which tacitly deny a historian's right to give summary accounts of transactions or choose his incidents according to his purpose in writing. Any careful examination of the passages involved will prove not only that they are not inconsistent, but rather mutually supplementary accounts;* but also that they actually imply

* The events recorded by Luke are—1. Annunciation

ɔne another, and prove the truth of each other by a series of striking undesigned coincidences.*

to Zachariah; 2. Annunciation to Mary (in the sixth month thereafter); 3. Mary's visit to Elizabeth (extending to three months later); 4. Birth of John (after 3); 5. His circumcision (eight days after 4); 6. Journey of Joseph and Mary to Bethlehem ("in those days"); 7. Birth of Jesus (while at Bethlehem); 8. Annunciation to the shepherds (the same day); 9. Visit of the shepherds (hastening); 10. Circumcision of Jesus (eight days after); 11. Presentation (thirty-three days later); 12. Return to Nazareth (when all legal duties were performed). The events recorded by Matthew are—A. Mary is found with child (before she is taken to Joseph's house); B. Annunciation to Joseph; C. Mary is taken home by Joseph; D. Visit of the Magi (after Jesus' birth at Bethlehem); E. Flight into Egypt (after their departure); F. Slaughter of the innocents (when Herod had discovered that the wise men had gone); G. Death of Herod; H. Return from Egypt to Nazareth (after Herod's death). These events dovetail beautifully into one another, as follows: 1, 2, 3, 4, 5, A, B, C, 6, 7, 8, 9, 10, 11, D [12 (E, F, G, H)]. It is only necessary to assume that 12 includes E, F, G and H compendiously, and all goes most smoothly. Other arrangements are also possible—e. g. the first half may bᴇ varied to 1, 2, A, B, C, 3, 4, 5, 6, or to 1, 2, A, 3, B, C, 4, 5, 6; and the second half to 9, 10, D, 11 [12—(E, F, G, H)], or even to 9, 10, D, E, F, G, half H, 11, half H—12. In the face of so many possible harmonizations it certainly cannot be asserted that harmony is impossible.

* Thus the account in the one of the annunciation to

And when it is added that the choice of the material which each writer has made can in each incident be shown to have arisen directly out of the purpose of the writer, it may be seen what a load the assertion of disharmony must carry.

Joseph, and that in the other of that to Mary, which are often said to be irreconcilable with one another, actually prove each other's truth. Both assume exactly the same facts at their bases—viz. that Mary conceived a child supernaturally, and remained a virgin while becoming a mother. Moreover, if Luke's narrative be true, then something like what Matthew records must have happened; and if Matthew's be true, something like what Luke records must have happened. Two things needed explanation: why Mary was not crazed at finding herself so strangely with child, and how Joseph, being a just man, could have taken her, in that condition, to wife. Luke's narrative explains the first, but leaves the other unexplained; Matthew's explains the second, but leaves the first unexplained. It is admitted that there was no collusion here. How does it happen, then, that the two so imply one another? Again, Matthew does not mention where Jesus' parents lived before his birth, but only states that after that birth they intended to live in Bethlehem, and, after having been deterred from that, chose Nazareth. Now, why this strange choice? Luke, and Luke alone, supplies the reason: Nazareth was their old home. Still, again, that Luke calls Mary Joseph's "betrothed" in ii. 5 is not only remarkable, but totally inexplicable from Luke; we can only understand it when we revert

The asserted contradiction between Acts and Galatians is already crumbling of its own weight. Thus Keim, certainly no very "apologetic" critic, has shown very clearly that the passage in Galatians has suffered much eis-egesis in order to make out the disharmony,[*] and sober criticism will judge that even he has done inadequate justice to the subject. We cannot enter into details in so broad a question : it will be sufficient, however, to call attention to the fact that no disharmony can be made out unless—(1) Violence be done to the context in Galatians, where Paul professes to be giving an exhaustive account, *not* of his visits to Jerusalem, *but* of his opportunities to learn from the apostles. Any visit undertaken at such a time as to furnish no such opportunity (and Acts xii. was such) ought, therefore, to have been omitted. (2) Convenient forgetfulness be exercised of the fact that while the context shows that Paul uses " apostles " in the narrow sense in Gal. i. 19, yet this is not true of Acts ix. 27 ; but, as Luke's usage shows, the contrary may very well be true (Acts xiv. 4, 14). So that it is in no sense inconsistent for Paul to say that he saw but one apostle, and

to Matt. i. 25 and the preceding verses. These are but samples.

[*] In *Aus der Urchristenthum* (1878).

Luke that he saw several. (3) Misunderstanding be fallen into as to the nature of the "decree" of Acts xv. 20, and its binding force to churches not yet formed and not parties to the compromise. (4) Misrepresentation be ventured as to the testimony of Galatians as to Paul's relations to the Twelve, which Paul represents to have been most pleasant (Gal. ii. 3, 7–10), but which are made out to have been unpleasant through misinterpretation of phrases in Gal. ii. 2, 3, 4, 6, 9, etc. (5) Incredible pressure of the detailed language of both Galatians and Acts be indulged in. (6) And, finally, a tacit denial be made of the possibility of truth subsisting through differences in choice of incidents arising from the diverse points of view of the two writers. In other words, an unbiased comparison of the two accounts brings out forcibly the fact that there is no disharmony between them at all. Taking these examples as samples (and they are certainly fair samples), it is as clear as daylight that no single case has as yet been adduced where disharmony is a necessary conclusion. Therefore all charges from this side fall to the ground:

6

CORRECT APPLICATION OF THE OLD TESTAMENT.

3. Another favorite charge against the **exact** truth of the New-Testament Scriptures is drawn from the use of the Old Testament in the New, and especially the phenomena of its quotation. Here also, however, most of the objections urged prove nothing but a radical lack of clear thinking on the part of those who bring them. For instance, Dr. Davidson argues * that the verbal variation which the New-Testament writers allow themselves in quoting the Old Testament is conclusive against verbal inspiration, for "the terms and phrases of the Old Testament, if literally inspired, were the best that could have been adopted," and therefore the New-Testament writers "should have adhered to the *ipsissima verba* of the Holy Spirit (seeing they were the best) as closely as the genius of the Hebrew and Greek languages allowed." Here, however, a false view of inspiration is presupposed, and also a false view of the nature and laws of quotation. Inspiration does not suppose that the words and phrases written under its influence are the best possible to express the truth, but only **that** they are an adequate expression of the

* *Hermeneutics*, p. 513.

truth. Other words and phrases might be equally adequate—might furnish a clearer, more exact, and therefore better, expression, especially of those truths which were subordinate or incidental for the original purpose of the writing. Nor is quotation to be confounded with translation. It does not, like it, profess to give as exact a representation of the original, in *all* its aspects and on *every* side, as possible, but only to give a true account of its teaching in *one* of its bearings. There is thus always an element of application in quotation; and it is therefore proper in quotation so to alter the form of the original as to bring out clearly its bearing on the one subject in hand, thus throwing the stress on the element in it for which it is cited. This would be improper in a translation. The laws which ought to govern quotation seem, indeed, to have been very inadequately investigated by those who plead the New-Testament methods of quotation against inspiration. We can pause now only to insist—(1) That quotation, being essentially different from translation, any amount of deviation from the original, *in form*, is thoroughly allowable, so long as the sense of the original is adhered to; provided only that the quoter is not professing to give the exact form; (2) That any adaptation of the original to the purpose in hand is allowable, so long as it proceeds by a true exegesis, and thus does not falsify the original; (3) That any neglect of the context of the original is allowable, so long as the purpose for which the quotation is adduced does not imply the context, and no falsification of sense is involved. In other words, briefly, quotation appeals to the sense, not the wording, of a previous document, and appeals to it for a definite and specific end; any dealing with the original is therefore legitimate which does not falsify its sense in the particular aspect needed for the purpose in hand.*   The only question which is relevant here, then, is, Do the New-Testament writers so quote the Old Testament as to falsify it?

Many writers who have pleaded the phenomena of the New Testament against verbal inspiration yet answer this question in the nega-

---

* Still further: the amount of freedom with which a document is dealt with will be greater in direct proportion to the thoroughness with which it is understood. If a quoter feels doubtful as to his understanding of it, he will copy it word for word; if he feels sure he understands it fully and thoroughly, he will allow himself great freedom in his use of it; and if he is the author of the original document, still more.   If he is conscious of having supernatural aid in understanding it, doubtless the amount of freedom would be greatest of all.

tive. Thus, Mr. Warington admits that there are " no really inapposite quotations "—" the pertinency of the quotations may be marred by their inaccurate citation, but pertinent, notwithstanding, they always are. In a word, while . . . the letter is often faulty, the spirit is always divinely true." * This is simply to yield the only point in debate. Others, however, of not such clearness of sight, do not scruple to assert that the New-Testament writers do deal so loosely with the Old Testament as to fall into actual falsification, and this mainly in two particulars: they quote passages in a sense different from that which they bore in the Old Testament, and they assign passages to wrong sources.

As an example of those who make the first charge we may take Prof. Jowett, who is never weary of repeating it. † But when we ask for his proof, it is found to rest on four false assumptions, tacitly made : that difference in form means difference in sense, that typology is a dream, that application through a true exegesis is illegitimate, and that all adoption of language binds one to its original sense. Thus Prof. Jowett has difficulty in finding apposite examples,

* *Inspiration*, p. 107.

† See *St. Paul's Epp.*, etc., vol. i., p. 353 *sq.*: London, 1855.

and those he does finally fix upoṇ fail on examination.*   Dr. Sanday, in his excellent class-

* The following are his examples: Rom. ii. 24, "where
the words are taken from Isaiah, but the sense from Ezekiel." Possibly a true criticism; what is illegitimate in it?
Note, however, that this is probably not a formal quotation, but an expression of Paul's own thought in Old-Testament words, and hence the "as it is written" succeeds
(not precedes) the quotation; this "as it is written" may
therefore refer to Isaiah as quoted, or to Isaiah and
Ezekiel, or to Ezekiel alone, now remembered by the
apostle.   (Compare Beet with Philippi Meyer *in loc.*)
Rom. ix. 33, where only a composition of two passages
takes place, which are rightly "harmonized," as Prof. J.
admits, in Christ. 1 Cor. iii. 19, where the words are
altered from the Psalm to suit the context indeed, but
also in direct agreement with their context in the Psalm,
so that no alteration in *sense* results. Rom. x. 11, which
is called an "instance of the introduction of a word [$\pi\tilde{\alpha}\varsigma$]
on which the point of the argument turns," but which
is simply a case of true exegesis and application to the
matter in hand. The same passage, and without the
$\pi\tilde{\alpha}\varsigma$, had already been quoted in this context (ix. 33);
Paul now requotes it, calling attention to the force of the
unlimited $\dot{o}$ $\pi\iota\sigma\tau\epsilon\dot{\upsilon}\omega\nu$ by emphasizing its sense through an
introduced $\pi\tilde{\alpha}\varsigma$, and confirming his interpretation immediately by an additional Scripture (verse 13).   Compare
Luke xviii. 14, as given in Matt. xxiii. 14, as an example of like explanation. 1 Cor. xvi. 21, which is admitted to be a case "of addition rather than alteration,"
and any objection to which must rest on a tacit denial
of typology, which even Meyer admits to be historically

ification of New-Testament quotations as to

justifiable here. Rom. x. 6–9, presenting alterations
which "we should hesitate to attribute to the apostle but
for other examples, which we have already quoted, of
similar changes," but which, even if considered as a
quotation, is defensible enough; then how much more
so when we note that it does not profess to be a quotation, and is probably nothing more than the expression
of the apostle's thought in old and beloved words!
1 Cor. xv. 45, " a remarkable instance of discrepancy
in both words and meaning from Gen. ii. 7." Quite
true, and therefore neither in words nor meaning taken
from Gen. 7. Prof. J. has simply neglected to note that
the quotation extends only to ζῶσαν. (Cf. Meyer *in loc.*)
Rom. x. 13, where the charge of change of meaning
rests only on a misunderstanding of Mal. i. 2, 3. Rom.
iii. 10 *sq.*, " a cento of quotations transferred by the
apostle [from their original narrow reference] to the
world in general." As if Eccles. vii. 21, Ps. xiii. (xiv.)
12 were not already as universal as anybody could make
them, and as if the choice of passages throughout was
not admirably adapted to Paul's purpose, which was to
prove that all men are sinners—yes, even the Jews.
Rom. xii. 20, which requires no remark. And finally
six allegories, which are immediately admitted not to be
allegories in the only sense of the word which would be
to their disadvantage—*i. e.* in the sense of an interpretation which treated the literal sense of the words as
unimportant, in which sense of the word no allegory
occurs in the New Testament. These "allegories" are,
some of them, simple illustrations, some *typical* inter-
pretations.

their form,* cites two passages only which can
be plausibly asserted to be cases of mistaken
ascription—viz. Mark i. 2 and Matt. xxvii. 9,
10. The first of these ought not to present
any difficulty. The form of the sentence shows
that the actual words of the citation are paren-
thetical in essence: Mark declares that John
came preaching in accordance with a prophecy
of Isaiah, and then inserts, parenthetically, the
words referred to, adding also a parallel prophecy of Malachi. That he gives more evidence
than he promised ought surely to be no objection; it is enough that, having promised a
prophecy from Isaiah, he does give it. This
is strengthened by the fact that the prophecy
quoted from Malachi is actually based on, and
largely drawn out of, Isaiah, so that Isaiah is
actually the ultimate source of both the prophecies given, and that from Malachi can be rightly looked upon as simply a further explanation
of what is essentially Isaiah's. The quotation in
Matt. xxvii. 9, 10, on the other hand, does present a difficulty, and is indeed, in whatever aspect it be looked upon, a very puzzling case. It
presents the extreme limit of paraphrase of the
original, and it is exceedingly difficult to assign
all its parts to their proper originals. It is plain,

* *Gospels in the Second Century,* pp. 16–25.

however, that Zech. xi. 13 was strongly coloring
the writer's thoughts when he wrote it. Yet he
ascribes it to Jeremiah. Here, it is said, is a
clear case of erroneous ascription. This judgment, however, takes no account of the exceed-
ing difficulty of ascribing the words actually
quoted to Zechariah alone. There seem to be
but three ways in which the passage can be
plausibly understood, and no one of these implies
an error on Matthew's part. We may either (1)
understand the words as a very free paraphrase
of Zech. xi. 13, and then appeal to the fact that
in the Talmudic arrangement Jeremiah stood
first in the " book of the prophets," so that Jeremiah here stands as general title for the whole
book—with Lightfoot, Scrivener, Cook, Schaff-
Riddle, etc. ; or (2) take the reference in v. 9 as
intended for Jer. xviii., xix.—apart from which
passage, indeed, the quotation following cannot
be understood—and suppose the quotation itself
to be deflected to the words of Zechariah, so that
the passage becomes analogous to Mark i. 2, and
is meant to call attention to both Jeremiah and
Zechariah — with (in general) Hengstenberg,
Hofmann, Thrupp, Fairbairn, etc,; or (3) we
may, with Lange, find the originals of the words
in four passages in Genesis, Zechariah and Jer-

emiah, the key to the whole being Jer. xxxii. 6–
8.   Whichever of these views may be accepted
is of no moment so far as the present question
is concerned ; each alike is consistent with the
evangelist's truth, and therefore with his inspiration.

With these examples we must close. It is
only necessary to add the caution that the passages dealt with are supposed by Mr. Jowett and
Dr. Sanday to be the most striking and difficult
ones that could be put to the apologist out of the
two hundred and seventy-eight quotations which
the New Testament makes from the Old. It is
surely not presumptuous, then, to assert that Mr.
Warington's wisdom is apparent, and that it is
true that the New-Testament quotations always
preserve the sense of the Old-Testament passages.

And with this, this paper must close. It has
been possible, of course, to examine only samples of critical objection. But those that have
been examined are samples, and have been select-
ed wholly in the interests of the objection. These
laid, therefore, and all are laid. The legitimate
proofs of the doctrine, resting primarily on the
claims of the sacred writers, having not been
rebutted by valid objections, that doctrine stands

doubly proved. Gnosis gives place to epignosis, faith to rational conviction, and we rest in the joyful and unshaken certainty that we possess a Bible written by the hands of men indeed. but also graven with the finger of God.

Appendix 1

INSPIRATION OF THE SCRIPTURES: FACING THE ISSUE

Benjamin B. Warfield

I was greatly surprised (not to say shocked) to read in an editorial, published under the above caption in your issue of July 30th, the following words: "In the April number of the *Presbyterian Review* Drs. A. A. Hodge and Warfield published an article defending the theory of *Plenary Verbal Inspiration*, after having reduced it, as we understand their position, to that of mere providential superintendence over its external production, and claiming this to be the true church doctrine."[1] This is followed by the double hint that that article has probably "let down the claims of inspiration too low,"[2] and that Princeton and Allegheny Seminaries are involved in the question.[3] This last point forces me to ask you to admit into your paper a few words from me in correction of the whole statement. While this would be hardly worth your while if only I personally were concerned, yet when what is being taught as to

Note: In this letter to the *Presbyterian*, Benjamin B. Warfield answered an editorial that had appeared in the issue dated 30 July 1881. Warfield's letter appeared on page 5 of the 13 August 1881 issue.

1. *Presbyterian*, 30 July 1881, p. 10, col. 1.

2. Ibid., col. 2.

3. Ibid., col. 1.

Inspiration by one of her Professors in one of her chief seminaries is the question, the Church has a right to the facts. Allow me, therefore, to make the following remarks:

1. Whatever the author of the editorial in question may have read out of (or into) the *Presbyterian Review* article, I would like to assure your readers that I do hold, and according to my ability try to defend, the strictest doctrine of Plenary Verbal Inspiration, without having reduced it to any thing at all — except to *Plenary Verbal Inspiration.* Your readers may feel perfectly certain that the theory taught most of them by Dr. Archibald Alexander or Dr. Charles Hodge — the doctrine defended in that so much abused and so much misrepresented little book of Gaussen's — is the theory taught, from the Scriptures and as scriptural, in the prosecution of my work at Allegheny.

2. How any one could see in the *Presbyterian Review* article any lowering of the claims of inspiration, and especially the lowering asserted in your editorial, simply amazes me. That article does indeed state that, although not mere superintendence, yet, in essence, Inspiration is of the nature of superintendence, rather than, say, of dictation.[4] But this is poles away from stating that it is *"mere providential* superintendence over the external production of scripture." Where in the world did the writer of the editorial get that "mere"? And where in the world did he get that "providential"? Not out of the article; they are carefully excluded by the article. The article carefully defines Inspiration to be, *not* "providential leading," *nor* "spontaneous human action,"

4. "Inspiration," *Presbyterian Review* 2 (1881): 226 / *Inspiration* (Philadelphia: Presbyterian Board of Publication, 1881), pp. 6-7.

but "a controlling influence from without";[5] *not* a thing "including historic processes and the concurrence of natural and supernatural forces," *but* a special "super- intendence by God in the entire process *of writing.*"[6] The article explains at great length that while the di- vine agency in the production of the Scriptures has en- tered it in various ways and forms — of providential guidance, spiritual illumination, direct revelation, and otherwise — yet all this was not Inspiration, but prelimi- nary thereto.[7] Inspiration was, in addition to all this, the special divine superintendence given to "secure the errorless expression in language of the thoughts de- signed by God."[8] The article declares that the Scrip- tures not only contain, but *are* the Word of God;[9] and that they, "in all their elements and all their affirma- tions, are absolutely errorless and binding."[10] The whole article is, indeed, a defense of the strictest theory of Verbal Inspiration, without any lowering at all.

3. And the issue raised by it is just this issue: the truth of the doctrine of Verbal Inspiration, the affirma- tive of which the article supports. So Dr. Briggs, for in- stance, understands it. He differs from it in that it teaches the "theory of Verbal Inspiration," and that the Scriptures claim to be so inspired as to preclude the pos- sibility of error in them.[11] Therefore Dr. Briggs' an-

5. Ibid., p. 225, line 16 / p. 5, line 20.

6. Ibid., p. 226, line 1 / p. 6, line 12.

7. Ibid., pp. 228-29 / 11-13.

8. Ibid., p. 231, line 28 / p. 16, line 23.

9. Ibid., p. 237 / 26.

10. Ibid. et passim.

11. "Critical Theories of the Sacred Scriptures in Relation to Their Inspiration: I. The Right, Duty, and Limits of Biblical Criticism," *Princeton Review* 2 (1881): 551, line 14 from bottom.

swering paper is throughout an argument against the strict doctrine of Verbal Inspiration.

In closing, I must state that I have written this without any consultation with Dr. Hodge, and that therefore I cannot show what answer (or *no answer*) he may prefer to give to your misapprehension of the drift of the article, in the preparation of which he allowed me to join with him. But I may be permitted to say that I know that he, as well as I, in that paper had it near his heart to defend the old, traditional church doctrine (I repeat, in full knowledge of what Dr. Briggs has written, that it is the church doctrine) of Verbal Inspiration; and that he, as well as I, cannot fail to be deeply pained that it was capable of being so grievously misunderstood as you have shown, by your editorial, that it can be.

Appendix 2

THE TRUTH ON INSPIRATION

Benjamin B. Warfield

Controversy should have small place in the *Truth*. The diffusion of Christian knowledge, the enkindling of Christian emotion, are ends much more consonant with its aims. It justly allows, however, some space to the discussion of the "all-important subject" of the inspiration of the Scriptures, by which the present writer understands the true doctrine of plenary verbal inspiration, and which he too esteems too precious to permit himself to be described as opposing it without entering his correction. His attention has been only just now called to a paper in the *Truth*, in which strictures are passed on a paper on Inspiration, by Dr. A. A. Hodge and himself, which was published in the *Presbyterian Review* for 1881. He consequently frankly asks the *Truth* to observe that it has been possible to make that paper appear liable to those strictures only by a very severe treatment of its language, amounting to an imposition of a foreign meaning upon it, instead of an exposition of its proper sense. He confidently expects of the *Truth* to permit him to correct the impression its readers may have received from the publication of the strictures.

Note: This article by Benjamin B. Warfield appeared in the *Truth* 9 (1883): 124-29 in response to James H. Brookes, "Inspiration," *Truth* 8 (1882): 490-95.

The *Presbyterian Review* article had said:

It must be remembered that it is not claimed that the Scriptures, any more than their authors, are omniscient. The information they convey is in the forms of human thought, and limited on all sides. They were not designed to teach philosophy, science or human history as such. *They were not designed to furnish an infallible system of speculative theology. They are written in human languages, whose words, inflections, constructions and idioms bear everywhere indelible traces of human error. The record itself furnishes evidence that the writers were in large measure dependent for their knowledge upon sources and methods in themselves fallible, and that their personal knowledge and judgments were in many matters hesitating and defective, or even wrong.* Nevertheless, the historical faith of the Church has always been that all the affirmations of Scripture of all kinds, whether of spiritual doctrine or duty, or of physical or historical fact, or of psychological or philosophical principle, are without any error, when the *ipsissima verba* of the original autographs are ascertained and interpreted in their natural and intended sense. There is a vast difference between exactness of statement, which includes an exhaustive rendering of details, an absolute literalness, which the Scriptures never profess, and accuracy, on the other hand, which secures a correct statement of facts on principles intended to be affirmed. It is this accuracy and this alone, as distinguished from exactness, which the Church doctrine maintains of every affirmation in the original text of Scripture without exception. Every statement accurately corresponds to truth just so far forth as affirmed.

The italicized portion of this section, the *Truth* singles out for attack as being rash, untrue and hopelessly inconsistent with the infallibility and divine inspiration of the Scriptures. The careful reader who will glance at it in its context may be trusted to take another view of it. It is to be observed that it is a portion of a rejoinder to the rather common objection to verbal inspiration, that it makes the human authors of the Bible *omniscient*. No, it says, verbal inspiration only supposes *errorlessness* in what is actually said. Men may pick flaws in the language used by the sacred writers — may show that the Greek of the Apocalypse, for example, is far removed from the purity of the Greek of Plato — may prove that new and strange words, late and un-attic inflections, solecistic constructions, and queer and uncouth, nay even — if literally pressed — false idioms (such as the idiom which made "the whole world" equivalent only to "the Roman world," Rom. 1:8) appear on the sacred pages: but the infallibility of the Bible and its divine authority are not thereby touched. Men may point out that Luke (Luke 1:3) obtained his knowledge of the facts recorded in his history just as Mr. Freeman or Canon Stubbs obtains his, and that the prophets misunderstood their messages, nay, that Peter could err in his judgment in an important action (Gal. 2:11 sq.); in neither case would objection rise against inspiration. Whatever may be the character of their Greek, however much words and idioms are used in other than their original senses: the intended sense shines clearly through, and this intended sense is divinely true. However the scripture writers obtained their knowledge, whether from divine revelation, or historical research, or personal experience, what they express is always true and accurate knowledge. However much they did not know, however wrong they may have been in their notions on many points whatever they set down in their books, and

thus actually teach, is found to be absolute fact. In fine,
however human they may have been in other respects,
so far forth as they affirm anything, every statement accurately corresponds to truth. This is what verbal inspiration means; it does not hold that what the sacred
writers *do not affirm* is infallibly true, but only that
what *they do affirm* is infallibly true. What is there in
this rash or untrue or inconsistent with the infallibility
of the Bible? It is a defense of that infallibility.

Yet how does the *Truth* deal with it? It says:

> If Profs. Hodge and Warfield mean that the words
> *of Scripture* "bear everywhere indelible traces of
> human error," and that the sacred writers *in their*
> *scriptural statements* "were in large measure
> dependent for their knowledge upon sources and
> methods in themselves fallible, and that their per-
> sonal knowledge and judgments [*as to anything*
> *they wrote*] were in many matters hesitating and
> defective, or even wrong," it might be sufficient
> to quote their own language in the same article
> against themselves: "this view gives up the whole
> matter of the immediate divine authorship of the
> Bible as the word of God, and its infallibility and
> authority as a rule of faith and practice."

Three of the clauses above have been italicized by
me. It will be observed that it is on them that the harsh
criticism hangs. It will be observed also that no one of
them is justified by the article criticized. Let the reader
turn back to the former extract and note the second of
its italicized sentences. He will quickly see that the
antecedent of "whose" is *not* "scripture" *but* "human
languages." It is one thing to say that all human language bears indelible traces of human error; another for
the *Truth* to transmute this into the statement that
Scripture bears such traces. The reader will look in vain

also for the other italicized clauses in the criticized article, the very opposite of which he will on the contrary
find. It is not meant of course to charge the *Truth* with
intentional misrepresentation; but has not a grievous
wrong been done through careless misrepresentation?
The authors of the article criticized certainly wish to be
understood in a sense diametrically opposite to that
which the *Truth* reads into their words; and the present
writer may be allowed to state that he thinks those
words an admirably clear statement of that opposite
sense, when he confesses in the same breath that, although he could heartily have wished to be, he is not actually their author.

There seems to be no call for a defense of the other
passage upon which the *Truth* animadverts adversely:
not because it is not both true and important, but for
four reasons: (1) It is not charged with "error" but only
with "nonsense." (2) It shares that "nonsense" with all
recent writers of repute on inspiration (e.g. Bannerman,
Dr. Chas. Hodge, Breckinridge, Patton, etc.). (3) Even
the careless reader will not fail to note that the charge
is due to an unfortunate confusion on the part of the re-
viewer of Inspiration with Revelation, so that he understands of the latter what is affirmed of the former alone.
And (4) it is much nearer the heart of the present writer
to close with a word to the readers of the *Truth* which
may strengthen their faith in the glorious truth of an inspired Bible than it is to prove that Dr. Hodge and
himself do not write "nonsense." That we have an inspired Bible and a verbally inspired one, we have the
witness of God Himself; and that this means that every
statement of whatever kind in the whole compass of
Scripture, from the first word of Genesis to the last of
Revelation, is infallibly true and of absolute authority
to bind the head, heart, and life, rests on no lower

authority. The heart of God's people has in all ages responded to the fact with glad reverence. The hope of the world rests on it. It is the rock on which the confidence of our late age in the sufficiency of Christ's sacrifice and the surety of our salvation is built. May the man who through indifference, carelessness, conceit, or wickedness would deny this truth of God and teach men so — no, *not* perish — but be converted from the error of his way and, like a second Paul, be set by God's power and call to defend that which he would have destroyed.

Appendix 3

WARFIELD ON SCRIPTURE:
A CHRONOLOGICAL BIBLIOGRAPHY

Roger R. Nicole

Many of the following articles have been reprinted in one or more places. For a complete publishing history of each article, see *A Bibliography of Benjamin Breckinridge Warfield, 1851-1921* by John E. Meeter and Roger R. Nicole.[1]

1. "Inspiration and Criticism." In *Discourses Occasioned by the Inauguration of Benjamin B. Warfield to the Chair of New Testament Exegesis and Literature in Western Theological Seminary.* Pittsburgh, **1880.**
2. *The Divine Origin of the Bible.* Philadelphia: Presbyterian Board of Publication, **1882.**
3. "Inspiration and the Spurious Verses at the End of Mark." *Sunday School Times,* 20 January **1883,** pp. 36-37.
4. "The Descriptive Names Applied to the New Testament Books by the Earliest Christian Writers." *Bibliotheca Sacra* 42 **(1885):** 545-64.
5. Review of A. T. Pierson, ed., *The Inspired Word* (1888). *Presbyterian Review* 9 **(1888):** 511-12.
6. Review of Louis Gaussen, *Theopneustia: The Plenary Inspiration of the Holy Scriptures* (1888); Basil

1. Nutley, N.J.: Presbyterian and Reformed, 1974.

Manly, *The Bible Doctrine of Inspiration* (1888); George T. Ladd, *What Is the Bible?* (1888). *Presbyterian Review* 9 (**1888**): 672-77.

7. Review of Alfred Cave, *The Inspiration of the Old Testament* (1888). *Presbyterian Review* 10 (**1889**): 325-30.

8. Review of Robert F. Horton, *Inspiration and the Bible*, 2d ed. (n.d.). *Presbyterian Review* 10 (**1889**): 324-25. See also *Presbyterian and Reformed Review* 1 (1890): 514-15; 2 (1891): 162.

9. "Paul's Doctrine of the Old Testament." *Presbyterian Quarterly* 3 (**1889**): 389-406.

10. Review of A. W. Dieckhoff, *Das Gepredigte Wort und die Heilige Schrift* (1886) and *Das Wort Gottes* (1888). *Presbyterian Review* 10 (**1889**): 504-7.

11. "The Authority and Inspiration of the Scriptures." *Westminster Teacher* 17 (**1889**): 324-26.

12. "The Westminster Doctrine of Inspiration." *Independent* 41 (**1889**): 1605-6.

13. Review of William G. Blaikie et al., *Letters Related to the Dods and Bruce Cases* (1890). *Presbyterian and Reformed Review* 2 (**1891**): 348-49.

14. "The Westminster Doctrine of Holy Scripture." *New York Observer*, 23 April **1891**, p. 133. Cf. 35.

15. "The Westminster Doctrine of Inspiration." *Independent* 43 (**1891**): 595-96. Cf. 41.

16. "The Present Problem of Inspiration." *Homiletic Review* 21 (**1891**): 410-16.

17. "The Shortest Catechism." *Detroit Free Press*, 27 May **1891**. An examination of the views of Charles A. Briggs.

18. Review of Charles A. Briggs, *The Authority of Holy Scripture*, 2d ed. (1891) and related literature. *Presbyterian and Reformed Review* 2 (**1891**): 534-35.

19. Review of William Sanday, *Oracles of God* (1891). *Presbyterian and Reformed Review* 2 **(1891)**: 710-12.
20. Review of Andrew Archibald, *The Bible Verified* (1890). *Presbyterian and Reformed Review* 2 **(1891)**: 712-13.
21. Review of Joseph Henry Thayer, *The Change of Attitude Towards the Bible* (1891). *Presbyterian and Reformed Review* 3 **(1892)**: 174-75.
22. Review of Washington Gladden, *Who Wrote the Bible?* (1891). *Presbyterian and Reformed Review* 3 **(1892)**: 175-76.
23. Review of James H. Brookes, *Chaff and Wheat: A Defense of Verbal Inspiration* (1891). *Presbyterian and Reformed Review* 3 **(1892)**: 369.
24. Review of Robert Watts, *Dr. Briggs' Theology Traced to Its Organific Principle* (1892). *Presbyterian and Reformed Review* 3 **(1892)**: 373.
25. Review of Marvin R. Vincent, *Exegesis* (1891). *Presbyterian and Reformed Review* 3 **(1892)**: 375-77.
26. "The Rights of Criticism and of the Church." *Presbyterian,* 13 April **1892**, pp. 7-8.
— Proposed paper for the General Assembly at Portland, to be used in preferring charges against Dr. Briggs. 7 May **1892**. A manuscript located among the Warfield papers in Princeton Theological Seminary.
27. "Notes on the General Assembly of 1892." *Presbyterian and Reformed Review* 3 **(1892)**: 540-42. Deals with inerrancy.
28. Review of C. J. Ellicott, *Christus Comprobator,* 3d ed. (1892). *Presbyterian and Reformed Review* 3 **(1892)**: 763-64.
29. "The New Testament Use of the Septuagint, and Inspiration." *Presbyterian Journal* 17 **(1892)**: 786-87.

30. Review of Francis J. Sharr, *The Inspiration of the Holy Scriptures* (1891). *Presbyterian and Reformed Review* 4 (**1893**): 165-66.

31. Review of William Lee, *The Inspiration of Holy Scripture* (1892). *Presbyterian and Reformed Review* 4 (**1893**): 166.

32. "The Inerrancy of the Original Autographs." *Independent* 45 (**1893**): 382-83.

33. "The Real Problem of Inspiration." *Presbyterian and Reformed Review* 4 (**1893**): 177-221.

34. "Some Recent German Discussions on Inspiration." *Presbyterian and Reformed Review* 4 (**1893**): 487-99.[2]

35. "The Westminster Doctrine of Holy Scripture." *Presbyterian and Reformed Review* 4 (**1893**): 582-655. An expansion of 12 and 14.

36. Review of Randolph S. Foster, *Studies in Theology*, vols. 1-3 (1889-1890). *Presbyterian and Reformed Review* 4 (**1893**): 684.

37. "The Bible Doctrine of Inspiration." *Christian Thought* 11 (**1893**): 163-81.

38. "Dr. B. B. Warfield Replies to His Critics." *Christian Thought* 11 (**1893**): 215-19.

39. "Inspiration." In *Johnson's Universal Cyclopaedia*, edited by Charles Kendall Adams. New ed. 12 vols. New York: Johnson, **1893-1897**. 4:615-20.

---

2. This review article covers the following works: W. Rohnert, *Die Inspiration der Heiligen Schrift und ihre Bestreiter* (1889); Adolf Bolliger, *Das Schriftprinzip der Protestantischen Kirche* (1890); Wilhelm Koelling, *Die Lehre von der Theopneustie* (1891); idem, *Prolegomena zur Lehre von der Theopneustie* (1890); A. W. Dieckhoff, *Die Inspiration und Irrthumslosigkeit der Heiligen Schrift* (1891); P. O. Kier, *Bedarf es einer besonderen Inspirationslehre?* (1892); W. Fr. Gess, *Die Inspiration der Helden der Bibel und der Schriften der Bibel* (1892).

40. "Revelation." In *Johnson's Universal Cyclopaedia,* edited by Charles Kendall Adams. New ed. 12 vols. New York: Johnson, **1893-1897.** 7:79-81.

41. "The Doctrine of Inspiration of the Westminster Divines." *Presbyterian Quarterly* 8 **(1894):** 19-76. An expansion of 15.

42. Review of J. Paterson Smyth, *How God Inspired the Bible* (1892); John De Witt, *What Is Inspiration?* (1893); T. George Rooke, *Inspiration* (1893). *Presbyterian and Reformed Review* 5 **(1894):** 169-79.

43. "Theories of Inspiration." *Presbyterian Messenger* 1 **(1894):** 675-77. Cf. 39.

44. "The Divine and Human in the Bible." *Presbyterian Journal* 19 **(1894):** 280.

45. Review of E. Winter, *What Is Inspiration?* (1894). *Presbyterian and Reformed Review* 5 **(1894):** 544.

46. "The Westminster Confession and the 'Original Autographs.'" *Presbyterian Messenger* 1 **(1894):** 1181-82.

47. "Professor Henry Preserved Smith on Inspiration." *Presbyterian and Reformed Review* 5 **(1894):** 600- 653.

48. "The Inspiration of the Bible." *Bibliotheca Sacra* 51 **(1894):** 614-40.

49. "Theories of Revelation." *Presbyterian Messenger,* 20 December **1894,** pp. 7-8. Cf. 40.

50. Review of Frank Hallam, *The Breath of God* (1895). *Presbyterian and Reformed Review* 6 **(1895):** 559- 60.

51. Review of Marvin R. Vincent, *Biblical Inspiration and Christ* (1894). *Presbyterian and Reformed Review* 6 **(1895):** 560-62.

52. Review of James Denney, *Studies in Theology,* 2d ed. (1895). *Presbyterian and Reformed Review* 6 **(1895):** 784-85.

53. Review of John Urquhart, *The Inspiration and Accuracy of the Holy Scriptures* (1895). *Presbyterian and Reformed Review* 7 (**1896**): 365.

54. Review of William Sanday, *Inspiration,* 3d ed. (1896). *Presbyterian and Reformed Review* 7 (**1896**): 562-63.

55. "Introductory Note." In Abraham Kuyper, *Encyclopaedia of Sacred Theology.* New York: Scribner, **1898.** Pp. xi-xix.

56. "Inspiration." In *Bible Dictionary,* edited by John Davis. Philadelphia: Westminster, **1898.** Pp. 320-21.

57. Review of Th. Beyer, *Das A. T. im Licht des Zeugnisses Christi* (1897). *Presbyterian and Reformed Review* 9 (**1898**): 167-69.

58. Review of H. E. Ryle, *Philo and Holy Scripture* (1895). *Presbyterian and Reformed Review* 10 (**1899**): 154.

59. " 'It Says,' 'Scripture Says,' 'God Says.' " *Presbyterian and Reformed Review* 10 (**1899**): 472-510.

60. "Rothe's Consolation." *New York Observer,* 21 September **1899**, p. 358. A poem.

61. "God-Inspired Scripture." *Presbyterian and Reformed Review* 11 (**1900**): 89-130.

62. " 'The Oracles of God.' " *Presbyterian and Reformed Review* 11 (**1900**): 217-60.

63. "Errors and Blunders." *Bible Student* 1 (**1900**): 241-45.

64. Review of James R. Donehoo, *The New Testament View of the Old Testament* (1900). *Presbyterian and Reformed Review* 11 (**1900**): 553-54.

65. "Is the Bible the Word of God? The Acts." *Record of Christian Work* 19 (**1900**): 493-97. Cf. 21.

66. "Christianity and Revelation." *Bible Student* 5 (**1902**): 123-28.

67. Review of Howard Osgood, *Christ and the Old Testament* (1902). *Presbyterian and Reformed Review* 13 **(1902)**: 657.

68. Review of T. K. Cheyne, *Bible Problems and the New Material for Their Solution* (1904). *Princeton Theological Review* 3 **(1905)**: 674-78.

69. "Dr. Dods' Doctrine of Holy Scripture." *Bible Student and Teacher* 4 **(1906)**: 1-10.

70. Review of Charles S. MacFarland, *Jesus and the Prophets* (1905). *Princeton Theological Review* 4 **(1906)**: 120-21.

71. Adaptation of Balthazar Huebmaier's poem "The Everlasting Word of God." *Presbyterian*, 24 October **1906**, p. 9.

72. "Augustine's Doctrine of Knowledge and Author-
73. ity." *Princeton Theological Review* 5 **(1907)**: 353-97, 529-78.

74. Review of Albert Houtin, *La Question Biblique au XXe Siecle* (1906). *Princeton Theological Review* 5 **(1907)**: 659-64.

75. "Scripture." *Dictionary of Christ and the Gospels*, edited by James Hastings, vol. 2. New York: Scribner, **1908**. Pp. 584-87.

76. "Calvin's Doctrine of the Knowledge of God." *Princeton Theological Review* 7 **(1909)**: 219-325.

77. "Calvin and the Bible." *Presbyterian*, 30 June **1909**, pp. 7-8.

78. Review of William N. Clarke, *Sixty Years with the Bible* (1909). *Princeton Theological Review* 8 **(1910)**: 162-67.

79. "'Scripture,' 'the Scriptures' in the New Testament." *Princeton Theological Review* 8 **(1910)**: 560-612. An expansion of 75.

80. Review of Reinhold Seeberg, *Revelation and Inspiration* (1909). *Princeton Theological Review* 8 (1910): 679-88.
81. *The Bible the Book of Mankind*. New York: American Bible Society, 1915.
82. "Inspiration." In *The International Standard Bible Encyclopaedia*, edited by James Orr. 5 vols. Chicago: Howard-Severance, 1915. 3:1473-83.
83. "Revelation." In *The International Standard Bible Encyclopaedia*, edited by James Orr. 5 vols. Chicago: Howard-Severance, 1915. 4:2573-82.

Appendix 4

ANALYSES OF WARFIELD'S VIEW OF SCRIPTURE: A BIBLIOGRAPHY

Roger R. Nicole

Behannon, Woodrow. "Benjamin B. Warfield's Concept of Religious Authority." Dissertation, Southwestern Baptist Theological Seminary, 1963.

Counts, William Martin. "A Study of Benjamin B. Warfield's View of the Doctrine of Inspiration." Th.M. thesis, Dallas Theological Seminary, 1959.

Fuller, Daniel P. "Benjamin B. Warfield's View of Faith and History: A Critique in the Light of the New Testament." *Bulletin of the Evangelical Theological Society* 11 (1968): 75-83. Cf. later discussion between Fuller and Clark H. Pinnock in *Journal of the Evangelical Theological Society* 16 (1973): 67-72.

Gerstner, John H. "Warfield's Case for Biblical Inerrancy." In *God's Inerrant Word*, edited by John W. Montgomery. Minneapolis: Bethany Fellowship, 1974. Pp. 115-42.

Hoffecker, Andrew. "The Relationship Between the Objective and Subjective Elements in Christian Religious Experience: A Study in the Systematic and Devotional Writings of Archibald Alexander, Charles Hodge, and B. B. Warfield." Ph.D. dissertation, Brown University, 1970.

Krabbendam, Hendrick. "B. B. Warfield vs. G. C. Berkouwer on Scripture." In *Inerrancy: The Extent of*

Biblical Authority, edited by Norman L. Geisler. Grand Rapids: Zondervan, 1980.

Kraus, Clyde Norman. "The Principle of Authority in the Theology of B. B. Warfield, William Adams Brown, and Gerald Birney Smith." Ph.D. dissertation, Duke University, 1961.

Lindsay, T. M. "The Doctrine of Scripture: The Reformers and the Princeton School." *The Expositor*, 5th series, 1 (1895): 278-93.

Markarian, John Jacob. "The Calvinistic Concept of the Biblical Revelation in the Theology of B. B. Warfield." Ph.D. dissertation, Drew University, 1963.

Nicole, Roger R. "The Inspiration of Scripture: B. B. Warfield and Dr. Dewey M. Beegle." *The Gordon Review* 8 (1964-1965): 93-109.

Peter, J. F. "Warfield on the Scriptures." *Reformed Theological Review* 16 (1957): 76-84.

Torrance, T. F. Review of Benjamin B. Warfield, *The Inspiration and Authority of the Bible* (1948). *Scottish Journal of Theology* 7 (1954): 104-8.

Trites, Allison A. "B. B. Warfield's View of the Authority of Scripture." Th.M. thesis, Princeton Theological Seminary, 1962.

Appendix 5

CHARLES HODGE'S
VIEW OF INERRANCY

Roger R. Nicole

Some have argued that Charles Hodge did not adhere strictly to inerrancy, and that this constitutes a significant difference of emphasis between his view and that of his pupils Archibald A. Hodge and Benjamin B. Warfield.[1] To our knowledge the only apparent basis for this contention is a well-known passage in Charles Hodge's *Systematic Theology:*

> The errors in matters of fact which skeptics search out bear no proportion to the whole. No sane man would deny that the Parthenon was built of marble, even if here and there a speck of sandstone should be detected in its structure. Not less unreasonable is it to deny the inspiration of such a book as the Bible, because one sacred writer says that on a given occasion twenty-four thousand, and another says that twenty-three thousand, men were slain. Surely a Christian may be allowed to tread such objections under his feet.[2]

1. See, for example, Ernest R. Sandeen, *The Roots of Fundamentalism: British and American Millenarianism, 1800-1930* (Chicago: University of Chicago, 1970), pp. 125-27.

2. *Systematic Theology*, 3 vols. (New York: Scribner, 1871 1873), 1:170.

If this statement were found in isolation, it could perhaps be argued that Hodge held the Scripture *does in fact* contain some minute errors, which remain, however, incidental and irrelevant, as would be some specks of sandstone in the marble of the Parthenon. But the statement is found in a development in which specifically Hodge was concerned to assert that the Bible, being the Word of God, is "miraculously free from the soiling touch of human fingers." The first sentence that follows the above quotation makes this quite clear, for Hodge continued: "Admitting that the Scriptures do contain, in a few instances, discrepancies which *with our present means of knowledge, we are unable satisfactorily to explain,* they furnish no rational ground for denying their infallibility."[3]

This is furthermore in line with what Hodge said at other points: "The effect of inspiration was to preserve him [the sacred writer] from error in teaching."[4] "It is a theological conclusion . . . to infer that because a historian did not need to have the facts dictated to him, that therefore he needed no control to preserve him from error."[5] ". . . what the sacred writers said the Holy Ghost said."[6] "[Inspiration] is not confined to moral and religious truths, but extends to statements of facts, whether scientific, historical, or geographical. It is not confined to those facts the importance of which is obvious, or which are involved in matters of doctrine. It extends to everything which any sacred writer asserts to be

3. Italics ours.

4. Ibid., p. 155.

5. Ibid., p. 156.

6. Ibid., p. 160 and passim.

true."[7] "Paul could not err in anything he taught. . . ."[8] "It is, of course, useless to contend that the sacred writers were infallible, if in point of fact they err."[9] "Theories are of men. Facts are of God. The Bible often contradicts the former, *never the latter.*"[10]

All these statements, and many others that could be quoted, as well as Hodge's sense of being in line with Francis Turretin and Archibald Alexander, as well as Archibald A. Hodge's and Benjamin B. Warfield's sense of being in line with Charles Hodge, make it very evident, in our opinion, that the quotation advanced above does not conclusively prove that Charles Hodge admitted some slight original errors in Scriptures. Its meaning in keeping with the context must be simply that he was not deterred from confessing the infallibility of the Bible by *his* inability to provide a fully satisfactory explanation in every one of the cases where a discrepancy is alleged. In this light the analogy derived from the Parthenon must be deemed somewhat infelicitous since its ambiguity may seem to countenance some misunderstandings, but it can scarcely be legitimately pressed to the point where it is allowed to stand as the lone witness to a position which is expressly disclaimed or discountenanced in scores of places.

7. Ibid., p. 163.

8. Ibid., p. 165.

9. Ibid., p. 169.

10. Ibid., p. 171. Italics ours.

Appendix 6

THE WESTMINSTER CONFESSION
AND INERRANCY

Roger R. Nicole

It has been asserted that the Westminster Confession does not affirm the inerrancy of Scripture. One who has so argued is Jack B. Rogers, author of a voluminous thesis on *Scripture in the Westminster Confession.*[1]

Benjamin B. Warfield wrote two articles on the doctrine of Scripture found in the Westminster Standards,[2] in which he adduced sixty-six quotations from seventeen different members of the Westminster Assembly.[3] He also cited two quotations from the minutes and 153

1. *Scripture in the Westminster Confession: A Problem of Historical Interpretation for American Presbyterianism* (Grand Rapids: Eerdmans, 1967).

2. "The Westminster Doctrine of Holy Scripture," in *The Westminster Assembly and Its Work* (New York: Oxford University, 1931), pp. 155-257; "The Doctrine of Inspiration of the Westminster Divines," in *The Westminster Assembly*, pp. 261-333. The former appeared originally in 1893, the latter in 1894.

3. The seventeen are (with members of the committee on the confession asterisked): *John Arrowsmith — 8 quotations, William Bridge — 6, Anthony Burgess — 3, *Cornelius Burges — 1, Edmund Calamy — 2, Richard Capel — 6, Daniel Featley — 1, *George Gillespie — 3, *Thomas Goodwin — 2, John Lightfoot — 5, William Lyford — 5, *Herbert Palmer — 1, *Edward Reynolds — 4, *Samuel Rutherford — 9, William Twisse — 1, James Ussher — 1, John White — 8.

from John Lightfoot, whose view he singled out for special study in the second article. This constitutes a solid body of some seventy-five pages of quoted materials, not to speak of the extensive correlation given elsewhere between the Westminster Confession and John Ball's *Catechism* and James Ussher's *Body of Divinity*.[4] Specifically on the issue of biblical inerrancy, Warfield concluded that inerrancy was part of the Westminster doctrine.

It is surprising that in his thesis Rogers gave only a very cursory review of Warfield's work on the Westminster Standards, much briefer in fact than that devoted to the work of Charles A. Briggs,[5] although the latter was flawed by some incredibly inept mistakes such as interpreting as a "Westminster divine's own view what are really the words of his opponent."[6]

It seems incredible that Rogers judged he could safely bypass all the evidence amassed by Warfield, presumably on the grounds that some members of the assembly were not Aristotelian in their philosophical presuppositions and that our primary source of reference for an adequate interpretation of the Confession of Faith must be the members of the committee that drafted it, viz., Cornelius Burges, Thomas Gataker, Robert Harris, Charles Herle, Joshua Hoyle, Edward Reynolds, Thomas Temple, and the four Scots: Robert Baillie, George Gillespie, Alexander Henderson, and Samuel Rutherford.[7] But Warfield did quote from four of these and from three more who were also members of

4. "The Westminster Doctrine of Holy Scripture," pp. 177-90.

5. Rogers discussed Warfield's work on pages 38-43, Briggs's on pages 28-38.

6. *Scripture in the Westminster Confession*, p. 39.

7. Ibid., p. 40.

the committee: John Arrowsmith, Thomas Goodwin, and Herbert Palmer (as attested by the minutes and by Rogers himself elsewhere).[8] In any case the committee would hardly come forward with a draft representing a substantially different position from that espoused by the preponderance of the assembly members.

Specifically on the issue of inerrancy, on which so much controversy focuses and on which Rogers is so eager to secure for his own stance the support of the Westminster divines, it is noteworthy that Rogers has only two pages[9] and not a single quotation from a single member of the assembly. Nowhere in his entire thesis, as far as we are aware, did he advance even one text from a Westminster divine in which it is stated that a passage of Scripture is actually in error. Warfield, by contrast, had adduced numerous examples of the painstaking care that a man like Lightfoot had exercised in explaining seeming discrepancies in Scripture, even in matters apparently inconsequential.[10] It may be noted in passing that the more artificial and unconvincing a person's explanation sounds, the more clearly the explanation bears witness to the person's will to harmonize and consequently to his confidence that no error could possibly be ascribed to the original text.

Those who expressly claim that the Bible contains errors do not fail to point out where such may be found. It is not difficult to provide quotations to this effect in the writings of Clericus, Charles A. Briggs, Henry Preserved Smith, Llewelyn J. Evans, Dewey M. Beegle, Daniel P. Fuller, and others. If indeed any of the West-

8. Ibid., p. 155.

9. Ibid., pp. 305-7.

10. "The Doctrine of Inspiration of the Westminster Divines," pp. 311-32.

minster divines were in agreement with this view of
Scripture, how is it that they so utterly failed to make
any pronouncement to this effect, when they were
clearly as well aware of some of the biblical problems as
any of the later scholars? Is it likely that there are
ready and convincing statements of biblical errancy
made by the Westminster men and that neither Briggs
nor Rogers found any of them? Is it likely that having
found them, they failed to quote them? The presumption must remain that unless clearcut evidence to the
contrary is adduced, the Westminster divines held that
the canonical Scriptures, being "the Word of God written" (1.2), reflect the character of God "the author
thereof," "who is truth itself" (1.4), so that "by ... faith
a Christian believeth to be true whatsoever is revealed
in the Word, for the authority of God Himself speaking
therein" (14.2).

This type of approach, amply documented by Rogers
himself,[11] appears simply incompatible with the notion
of error. In the words of Leo XIII: "By its very nature,
inspiration not only excludes all error, but makes its
presence as utterly impossible as it is for God, the
supreme truth, to be the author of any error whatever."[12]

---

11. *Scripture in the Westminster Confession,* pp. 309-14.

12. "Providentissimus Deus," in *The Church Teaches* (St.
Louis: Herder, 1955), p. 51.

BIBLIOGRAPHY OF WORKS
CITED BY WARFIELD

Bartlett, Samuel C. "The Inspiration of the New Testament." *Princeton Review* 56 (January 1880): 23-56.

Beet, Joseph Agar. *A Commentary on St. Paul's Epistle to the Romans.* London: Hodder and Stoughton, 1878.

Cesnola, Luigi Palma di. *Cyprus: Its Ancient Cities, Tombs, and Temples: A Narrative of Researches and Excavations During Ten Years' Residence in That Island.* New York: Harper, 1878.

Davidson, Samuel. *Sacred Hermeneutics Developed and Applied: Including a History of Biblical Interpretation from the Earliest of the Fathers to the Reformation.* Edinburgh: Clark, 1843.

Farrar, F. W. *The Life and Work of St. Paul.* 2 vols. New York: Dutton, 1879.

Fisher, George Park. *The Beginnings of Christianity, with a View of the State of the Roman World at the Birth of Christ.* New York: Scribner, 1877.

Gaussen, Louis. *Theopneustia: The Bible: Its Divine Origin and Entire Inspiration, Deduced from Internal Evidence and the Testimonies of Nature, History, and Science.* Translated by David Dundas Scott. Glasgow: Blackie, 1861.

Jowett, Benjamin. *The Epistles of St. Paul to the Thessalonians, Galatians, Romans: With Critical Notes and Dissertations.* 2d ed. 2 vols. London: Murray, 1859.

Keim, Theodor. *Aus dem Urchristenthum: Geschichtliche Untersuchungen...* Zürich: Füssli, 1878.

Lee, William. *The Inspiration of Holy Scripture: Its Nature and Proof: Eight Discourses Preached Before the University of Dublin.* 4th ed. Dublin: Hodges and Smith, 1865.

McClellan, John Brown, trans. *The New Testament.... A New Translation on the Basis of the Authorized Version, from a Critically Revised Greek Text...* Vol. 1: *The Four Gospels...* London: Macmillan, 1875.

Meyer, H. A. W. *Critical and Exegetical Commentary on the New Testament.* Edited and translated by W. P. Dickson, W. Stewart, and F. Crombie. 20 vols. Edinburgh: Clark, 1873-1883.

————. *Kritisch exegetisches Handbuch über die Evangelien des Markus und Lukas.* Gottingen: Vandenhoeck and Ruprecht, 1867.

Oosterzee, J. J. van. *Christian Dogmatics: A Text-Book for Academical Instruction and Private Study.* Translated by John Watson Watson and Maurice J. Evans. 2d ed. London: Hodder and Stoughton, 1878.

Prochorus. *"Acta Joannis," unter Benutzung von C. v. Tischendorf's Nachlass.* Edited by Theodor von Zahn. Erlangen, 1880.

Rawlinson, George. *The Historical Evidences of the Truth of the Scripture Records Stated Anew, with Special Reference to the Doubts and Discoveries of Modern Times: Eight Lectures Delivered in the Oxford University Pulpit, in the Year 1859, on the Bampton Foundation.* Boston: Gould and Lincoln, 1873.

Sanday, William. *The Gospels in the Second Century: An Examination of the Critical Part of a Work Entitled "Supernatural Religion."* London: Macmillan, 1876.

Schürer, Emil. *Lehrbuch der neutestamentlichen Zeitgeschichte.* Leipzig: Hinrichs, 1874.

Tholuck, August. "The Citations of the Old Testament in the New." Translated by Charles A. Aiken. *Bibliotheca Sacra* 11 (1854): 568-616.

Townson, Thomas. *Discourses on the Four Gospels, Chiefly with Regard to the Peculiar Design of Each and the Order and Places in Which They Were Written, to Which Is Added an Inquiry Concerning the Hours of St. John, of the Romans, and of Some Other Nations of Antiquity.* Oxford: Clarendon, 1778.

Warington, George. *The Inspiration of Scripture: Its Limits and Effects.* London, 1867.

Westcott, Brooke Foss. *An Introduction to the Study of the Gospels.* 5th ed. New York: Macmillan, 1875.

_____. "St. John's Gospel." In *The Speaker's Commentary,* edited by F. C. Cook. *New Testament,* vol. 2, pp. v-xcvii, 1-307. New York: Scribner, 1880.

INDEX OF AUTHORS

105

INDEX OF SCRIPTURE

INDEX OF SCRIPTURE